PROPERTY SUCCESS INSIDER FORMULA

UNLOCK YOUR FINANCIAL FREEDOM

CALUM KIRKNESS

www.propertysuccessinsider.com

COPYRIGHT

Best Way to Connect And Keep In Touch:

Facebook Page: Property Success Insider

DEDICATION

This book is dedicated to both my late grandfathers, my father and my mother for their support, encouragement and lessons in property, business and life. Without them, this book would not have been possible.

I would also like to dedicate this book to all the people who refuse to settle for mediocracy and have the courage, strength and belief to take the enormous opportunities that are available to make a difference in the world.

ACKNOWLEDGEMENTS

There are many people who have made an impact in my life that I would like to thank. There are too many to mention individually, but there are a few who stand out as being the ones who have created a lifelong and positive lasting impression.

I would like to thank the following people for their support, guidance, inspiration and the lifelong positive impact that they have made on my life:

- My mother for her love and support.
- My late father for his support and teaching me his construction skills and knowledge.
- To both my late grandfathers for the lessons learned from their success in business and property.
- My wife for her love and support.
- My sister and brother and law for giving me a wonderful niece and nephew.
- My late aunt and uncle, Mr Arthur and Mrs Margaret Henderson, for their kind support over the years and during my time at University in Dundee.
- Mr Billy and Mrs Eileen Lee for their very kind support during my college year in Glasgow.
- To the following people who I have worked with, or for:
    - Alan Moar – Former Head of Building at Orkney Islands Council for his support, guidance and lessons in construction project management.
    - Henk Janssen – Former Managing Director at Pellikaan Construction for his support, guidance and lessons in business and construction design and build.
- To my school teachers who treated and taught me well:
    - (Primary School) Mrs Kathleen Hutchison, Mrs Margaret Flaws

- o (Secondary School). Mr Jim and Mrs Avril Cromarty, Dr John Ireland and Mr Jocky Wood
- To my good friends – Mr Edwin Fraser, Miss Putu Jeniari, and Mr Aly Miller – for their friendship and support.
- Finally, to everyone who I have met on my journey.

ABOUT THE AUTHOR

CALUM KIRKNESS is self-made property investor, developer, entrepreneur, public speaker and the founder and CEO of Property Success Insider Ltd and several other companies. He is an internationally recognised and respected property entrepreneur with over 30 years' experience in the property investment and development sector. Calum has invested significant sums in his own personal development to gain the knowledge and expertise from some of the best in terms of business, entrepreneurship, public speaking, property investment and development.

Calum developed a passion for property, business, money, wealth and freedom from a young age. After a difficult start in life, growing up with a father who was battling with alcohol addiction, financial resources were tight. This led Calum to realise the importance and value of money and mindset in having freedom. He began working, earning money and saving from the age of 12 and learned the power of the compound effect from seeing his savings grow from the interest being earned.

By the age of 23, Calum had saved enough funds to buy his first plot of development land, and began his property development journey and building up his own property portfolio. In the early years, Calum took a very hands-on hard work approach to achieving success, which led him to learn the lesson that exchanging your time for money is not scalable or good for your health and certainly not a route to achieving success and freedom. This led him to continue to invest significant time and money into his personal development to obtain the knowledge that successful people use to achieve success, which he now passes on in this book to help those striving for financial freedom and to live life on their terms.

Calum learned from a young age that property was the best and safest investment strategy to build a passive income and wealth and continues to invest and develop property. Calum now focuses much of his time on developing Property Success Insider into a property investment and development educational and training company, with ambitious plans for the future.

CONTENTS

INTRODUCTION

How would you like to create financial freedom for yourself and your family and live the life of your dreams, on your terms, using property investment as the vehicle to get you there? It is possible and I am going to share with you how to achieve it in this book.

You are clearly ambitious and someone who is looking for more in your life. This is a great thing and needed more today than ever before! People can no longer solely rely on the state, company or personal pensions to provide them with financial security in retirement. Also, why would you want to be stuck in a situation where you must wait until the state retirement age to have freedom from your job, when you could achieve financial and time freedom much earlier? I'm sure you would like to be able to do the things that you want, when you want, where you want and with who you want.

There is nothing wrong with looking to continuously grow as a person. Growth is one of our basic human needs, and our natural human desire for more helps keep us growing, young and alive.

The time is now! There has never been a time in history when it was more important to take full control of our own destiny and financial security than today. The good news is: it has never been easier to achieve financial freedom.

We are living in times of a rapidly-changing world, but one thing that never changes is that people need somewhere to live. The property market is changing, but the fundamentals remain the same and it is still possible to start today and build a successful property portfolio and business. This book will show you how to achieve and secure your financial freedom in language that is easy to follow and understand, with no unnecessary jargon or content.

Whether you are an existing amateur landlord and property investor or someone looking to get started in property investment and/or trading, let this book be your roadmap to jumpstart your property success and your journey to reach and enjoy financial freedom. This book will guide you through a step-by-step formula, showing you various property strategies that you can start to plan and implement immediately after you have finished reading.

With the Government's relentless assault on the buy-to-let sector in recent years, it is important to understand and be up to date with the changes in order to minimise or avoid their impact. I believe with the right knowledge property will always be the best investment that you will ever make, next only to investing in your own personal development.

Warren Buffett, the greatest living investor, says that the best investment that you can ever make is in yourself. It is good enough advice for me and something I have done and continue to do and gained positive results from. The fact that you are reading this book, indicates to me that you are someone who also understands the value of personal development.

> *"The Rules of The Property Game Have Changed and Continue to Change."*
> **– Calum Kirkness**

> *"The Good News Is, With Change Comes Opportunity."*
> **– Calum Kirkness**

> *"In Order To Survive In Today's Fast-Changing World, Having The Ability To Adapt Is Much More Important Than Having Strength."*
> **– Calum Kirkness**

What you have in your hands is the book of knowledge that I wish I had available at the beginning of my property investment journey.

This book is written for those who have the courage to seek the insights required in order to escape from the clutches of mediocrity and succeed in building the life of their dreams through property. I am not a professional writer, I am just someone who has a passion for property and success which I would like to share with others, and hopefully help them achieve financial freedom and live the life of their dreams on their terms.

I hope you are one of them.

CHAPTER 1

HOW MY JOURNEY IN PROPERTY BEGAN AND DEVELOPED

I was born with business and property in my DNA! My grandfather had his own building and property development company... my father followed in his father's footsteps... and then I followed the same path. Talk about history repeating itself!

It is said that what we are exposed to in the first seven years of our life shapes, to a large extent, who we become and how we live the rest of our life! Since I could first see, hear and walk, I was exposed to the property investment, development, building and construction world! I have fond memories of exploring my way around building sites in my early days, watching and listening to what was being done to develop the sites and properties in to what would become much-needed homes.

Me and my father   Me and my grandfather

My grandfather was a carpenter who started his own building company shortly after the Second World War. There was a shortage of accommodation and money at the time and he spotted an opportunity to provide a solution to the problem. After the War was over, the military started selling off the redundant accommodation buildings (the buildings were sold separately to the land). The buildings were timber frame and timber clad, and my grandfather's vision and solution was to buy these timber buildings, carve them up into house-size sections and transport and re-construct them on the customer's land to create a new family home.

Once all the timber frame, war-time buildings purchased by my grandfather had been converted into homes, he used the rewards from the venture to fund the next opportunity. By this time, the country was beginning to recover, people were starting to have money and were looking for new traditional-build family houses. He used the capital that he had accumulated to purchase green-field development land, in the main town and in the village where he lived (and where I was brought up) concentrating on building three-bedroom detached bungalows to sell. He continued with this strategy for many years with success until he retired. He also carried out building and construction work for customers to build bespoke one-off houses, and commercial and farm buildings, etc.

My grandfather had a great vision, an ability to spot opportunities and the courage to take risks.

"Grab Opportunities When They Come Along."
– Calum Kirkness

"Look For Solutions To Problems And Offer Them."
– Calum Kirkness

"The Bigger The Problem That You Can Solve, The Bigger The Reward."
– Calum Kirkness

"Trust Your Vision For The Future: Believe In The Magic Of Your Intuition And Go For It!"
– Calum Kirkness

When my father left school at the age of 15, he joined his father's building and property development company as a carpenter and joiner. He worked hard and learned a wide range of construction skills. He was popular and well-respected with the workforce but due to family dynamics, he left and went his own way starting his own building company when my grandfather retired. My father had the skills and the work ethic, but he didn't have the same vision and level of business acumen to see the opportunities that his father had.

Interestingly, several more of the military accommodation buildings that had been taken over in the main town by the local authority to provide affordable housing, had now become available for sale. Like his father, my father bought up some of these buildings, dismantled them and sold them off as sections. Times had changed and the opportunity that my grandfather had seen and taken was no longer the same. Instead of looking for new opportunities, my father spent most of his life trading his time for money, which is not a good strategy if you wish to be rich and have financial and time freedom in your life.

"Selling Your Time For Money
Will Never Make You Rich."
– Calum Kirkness

"Opportunities Don't Last Forever; They Need To Be
Taken When They Arise."
– Calum Kirkness

"Just Because An Opportunity Worked In The Past,
Doesn't Mean That It Will Work Now Or In The Future."
– Calum Kirkness

"If You Want To Be Rich, You Need To Create A Solution
To A Problem That Becomes A Money-Making Machine."
– Calum Kirkness

My passion for business, money and success was so great that I started working after school, and in my school holidays, when I was 12 years old. I worked for a neighbour who was starting up an oyster farm at the time. I was selling my time for money and being paid based on results for part of the work that I was doing. I was working long hours and some weeks earning more than a working man's wage. I also started my first entrepreneur JV venture at 13 years old, without understanding what it was at the time. I would take the scrap wood in my father's workshop and make small wooden wheelbarrows, which I then sold in the local craft shop on a 50:50 split on the selling price.

I saved up my money and learned the power of the compound effect from the interest that I was earning from my money in a savings account. Interest rates were high back in the eighties, and I was happy to see the benefit of my bank balance increasing each month, but I didn't realise it was the compound effect working in my favour. When I was 16, I made a big mistake and used a large part of my savings to buy a car to learn to drive in. I wasn't of age, but there were private places to learn. Then, aged 17, I made the same mistake again, but even bigger this time, by purchasing a new car with a loan. I had a passion for nice cars, which I had also inherited from my father and grandfather. That same amount of money that had been growing and compounding interest was now a depreciating liability, and the compound effect was now working against me!

> *"The Earlier In Life You Learn The Power Of The Compound Effect, The Earlier You Will Achieve Financial Freedom."*
> **– Calum Kirkness**

When I was 15, I left school, against my mother's wishes, and joined my father's building company as an apprentice carpenter and joiner. At the time, the UK economy was in recession, and inflation and interest rates were sky high, in double-digit figures. A far shadow from today's rates. Margaret Thatcher was Prime Minister and she introduced the Youth Training Scheme (YTS) to help young school leavers into apprenticeships. The government paid the apprentice £25 a week in year one, and 50% of the year was spent at the building college. In year two, the weekly allowance increased to £35, and 25% of the year was spent at building college. Then in year, three the employer paid the apprentice their weekly wage, which I think was around £48 from memory, and 100% of the year was spent on-site with the employer. This was my opportunity to leave school! I had taken a pay cut to do so as I was now earning less than what I had been earning from ages 13 to 15, but I believed it was good for my future.

My apprenticeship was a tough one and there were many arguments between me and my father, but I learned a lot of valuable skills and lessons during that time. I was fortunate that one of my father's main customers was a successful business man who was making a lot of money in a different sector, then investing his profits into purchasing large commercial premises in the main town and converting and renovating the buildings to form office, retail and residential units, for long-term rent. There was a lot of grant funding available at the time for converting and renovating property to create residential and self-catering accommodation. The company we were doing the work for was expert in gaining grant funding and they were building a money-making machine.

My grandfather's business model was to buy land, develop properties and sell them. I was now learning the buy, renovate and hold model of property investing.

When my apprenticeship was complete, I left my father's company and went to work for a different building company for period of around nine months before starting my own building and property development company.

Having a job as an employee is something that I have always struggled with. I am much happier when I am being an entrepreneur looking for opportunities and solutions to help others fix a problem.

"Life is Always Happening For Us, Not To Us."
– Calum Kirkness

"I Would Always Recommend Keeping Family And Business Separate."
– Calum Kirkness

"Having A Regular Job Will Never Make You Rich."
– Calum Kirkness

"Having A Regular Job Takes Away Your Freedom."
– Calum Kirkness

I was young, ambitious, motivated, driven and hungry for success and over the next few years, I worked crazy hours each week to build up my business. I had endless energy fuelled by ambition and positive stress!

In 1993, the opportunity came for me to purchase a plot of development land. I remember sitting in my lawyer's office, at the opposite side of the desk from him, going through the legal details of the land purchase. Throughout the process, I was thinking back to my grandfather's business model and success, as well as the success of the family that we had developed many properties for during my apprenticeship, and I was confident that I was making a good investment decision. The same plot today would be valued at around five times what it was valued at in 1993, and most of the capital growth happened between then and 2008. I am sure you will agree that a 500% return on your investment in 15 or even 25 years is an excellent result, and one that the stock market would struggle to match. This is not a one-off land opportunity or stroke of luck and I will share some more similar examples throughout the book.

Following the purchase of the land and developing the property, I made several big personal and business mistakes, which were difficult lessons to learn. One was overwork which led to burnout and breakdown. My ambition, hunger and drive for success that had been fueling my energy to work crazy hours had peaked and was now taking a heavy toll on both my mental and physical health. It was like driving around in a performance car one moment to sitting in one with a blown-up engine the next! I was suffering from deep depression, high levels of anxiety, chronic fatigue and a loss of self-belief and confidence. The business and property development had become a burden and I was no longer able to work. My business became dormant and the property development came to a standstill. Despite feeling burnt out, I was determined to hang on to my business and property and desperately searching for a way to get my health back on track. When you have abused your health and effectively blown up your engine, it doesn't matter how much fuel you try adding, you are going nowhere until you repair the engine. I have seen many entrepreneurs over the years making the same mistake that I made.

> *"Never Sacrifice Your Health In The Pursuit Of Wealth –*
> *When You Destroy Your Health To Make Money,*
> *You Will Lose Your Income And Have To Spend*
> *The Money You Made In The Process*
> *To Get Your Health Back And It's Not A Quick Process –*
> *Work Smarter Not Harder."*
> **– Calum Kirkness**

Fast-forward to Friday 1st September 1995 when I was sitting at home on the living room floor. I was feeling lost, tired, frustrated and desperate for answers and a solution. I was looking through the newspapers and Friday was jobs advertisement day. I thought I needed a new job in a new location to kickstart myself back into action! Jobs for carpenters were plentiful at the time and carpentry was what I knew – it was within my comfort zone. But I also knew deep inside me that it was not really the answer. Whilst looking through the newspaper, something caught my eye. It was an advertisement for last-minute places at Glasgow College of Building and Printing to Study HNC in Building Inspection and Supervision. Now this advert was instantly and directly talking to me!

My best friend, who had been with me through thick and thin over the years was with me, and he was never shy to share his opinion, so I thought I'd better ask for his advice on this idea. I explained that I had seen this advert to study for an HNC in Building Inspection and Supervision. He immediately replied "WHAT? You going to college? You are not clever enough; you left school at 15. And what about your business and property? You will end up losing everything and what will people think?!"

I sat in silence for a moment, thinking, 'These are valid points, BUT...'

And then I replied, "I have always listened to your advice in the past and look where it has got me! I am a complete wreck in every way!"

So I told my ego where to go on this occasion. I faced my fears and grabbed this opportunity. It turned out to be a good one.

> *"Be Careful When Listening To Your Ego, It Is There To*
> *Protect You, Not To Help You Create Success."*
> **– Calum Kirkness**

I called the college and was invited for an interview in person the following Tuesday. I went for the interview and was accepted. Success! The course was due to start the following Monday, 8th September 1996. I had just a few days to get back home, prepare my things, arrange accommodation and travel back to Glasgow. I managed to gather the strength and motivation to pull it all together.

> *"Never Underestimate Your Own Strength. You Are*
> *Much Stronger Than You Think."*
> **– Calum Kirkness**

> *"Our Environment Where We Live And Spend A Lot Of*
> *Time Has A Big Impact On The Rest Of Our Life And Our*
> *Success Or Failure."*
> **– Calum Kirkness**

College was the perfect opportunity for me at the time, and I am very grateful that I grabbed it. It got me out of my normal environment, I performed well and graduated with merit, which was the highest pass mark possible. It was a much-needed boost to my knowledge and confidence.

I was now making progress in the recovery of my health, but was still not fully fit and healthy, so I thought I would like to use my qualifications to get me entry to University. I applied to study BSc in Quantity Surveying at Abertay University in Dundee, and was accepted straight into year two due to my qualifications and industry experience. I settled in quickly and was performing well.

"Believe In Yourself And
Never Underestimate Your Abilities."
– Calum Kirkness

At the end of my first year at University, I got the opportunity to take a gap year and work as a Clerk of Works in the Major Works Building Department at the Orkney Islands Council (OIC). The Council was undertaking its largest capital works expenditure programme to date, and I was fortunate to be involved in several large new-build and several smaller commercial buildings. It was a great opportunity and learning experience for me.

During my time in the temporary Clerk of Works position, a full-time COW position came up and I was encouraged to apply for it. It seemed a great opportunity to have a safe, secure job and have a regular income with pension benefit. It made complete logical sense, so I applied for the job and got it. It soon became apparent that something wasn't right for me, and my health started to deteriorate again. I was left facing another tough decision: whether to go back to university and complete my degree in Quantity Surveying, or accept where I was. I knew deep inside that going back to university would be the right decision even if it didn't seem the right logical answer! I am very grateful that I made the choice to go back to University and complete my degree. If I hadn't taken this opportunity at the time, I am sure I would have always looked back with regret. One year later, I graduated with the BSc in Quantity Surveying with Distinction, which was the highest pass grade possible.

University Graduation – BSc in Quantity Surveying with Distinction

"Trust Your Intuition And Gut Feeling."
– Calum Kirkness

"Life Is Magical, Not Logical."
– Calum Kirkness

"We Can Only Make The Connections From Our Actions
And Experiences When Looking Back."
– Calum Kirkness

"Believe In Yourself, Believe In Your Dreams."
– Calum Kirkness

During my time at University and working for the OIC, I had managed to make progress and finish the house I was building. During this period, a local farmer who was retiring from his nearby farm, had approached me several times to see if I would sell the house. The first few times I was reluctant to sell, despite the property feeling like it was a heavy burden. I had made the mistake of investing too much of my own time, labour and emotion into building it. I carried out most of the works myself to save money, which meant that I had built the property at a low cost and on paper made a nice profit. I paid a high price though in terms of my health and lost several years' income, which was much more than the profit that I made from the house. I later agreed to sell the house to the farmer.

Looking back, I learned that there are different levels of motivation. Just because someone is not motivated to sell today, doesn't mean they won't become motivated later. This is valuable to understand when dealing with motivated sellers, which is covered later in the book.

My first project as a property developer. The house I sold to the retiring farmer.

"Leave Emotion out of investing decisions."

"One Of The Biggest Things That Holds Us Back Is Forming Attachment To Things."
– Calum Kirkness

"Let Go Of Anything That Is Weighing You Down And Move On."
– Calum Kirkness

"There Are Different Levels Of Motivation. A 'No' Today Does Not Mean A 'No' Tomorrow, Next Week Or Next Month."
– Calum Kirkness

"Always Follow Up On Leads Even After An Initial No Response."
– Calum Kirkness

Following the sale of my land and house, I thought to myself: 'There must be easier ways of making money than developing property!' I used the profits made from the house sale to invest in several different other asset classes. They were a mix of low, medium and high-risk investments that all turned out to be a complete or significant disaster.

After losing most of my money, I decided to cash in what was left, or what I could still access, and thought maybe property was not as bad after all! Over the next few years, I started to buy some development land again and took some big risks. The first site that I bought was a brownfield commercial site in the main town. The site was in a good, residential area with no other commercial buildings nearby. My plans for the site were to either turn the existing buildings into apartments, or knock down the buildings and build new residential apartments. I have since been offered eight times the value of what I paid for the site and plan to develop it myself soon.

A few years after purchasing the site, I submitted a planning application for eight apartments. The application received objections from the neighbours, which meant that it would need to be referred to a planning committee to decide. Despite the planning officers recommending the application to the committee for approval, the committee turned down the application and refused planning permission for the scheme that I had submitted.

Shortly after buying the development site just mentioned, I purchased another brownfield commercial site on the edge of a village. I could see the potential of this brownfield site, but it wasn't mortgageable as there was a block on development in the village until the mains sewer had been upgraded, which was thought to be a few years away, but turned out to be six years. It was a good location and I was determined to buy the site, so I bought it using three separate personal loans and paid significantly more than the market value at the time to secure it.

Once the main sewer had been upgraded, I secured planning consent for nine large, luxury apartments and a conference centre on the site. This all happened shortly before the peak of the market in 2008. I had everything in place to start, except for the structural engineer's certificate, which was delaying the final issue of the Building Warrant Approval. The structural engineering company that I appointed performed badly and took a long time to complete the design; way longer than the contract between us stated. Thankfully, I had a written and signed contract in place with them, which I had negotiated well.

"In My Experience, Property Investment Is The Best And Safest Investment."
– Calum Kirkness

"Buy Property Based On Location, Location, Location."
– Calum Kirkness

"Land Is An Excellent Investment And Tends To Rise In Value At A Higher Rate Than Property, But Generally Doesn't Produce Any Or Much Income Until Developed."
– Calum Kirkness

"There Is No Such Thing As Get Rich Quick."
– Calum Kirkness

"Planning Can Be A Political Process."
– Calum Kirkness

"Get All Contracts In Writing."
– Calum Kirkness

"The Greatest Risk In To Your Future Is Taking No Risk. When We Take No Risk, We Allow Fear To Dictate Our Future And Risking Everything."
– Calum Kirkness

Over the next few years, I also invested in buying off-plan and newly-completed properties, which have all been very good investment decisions. Some property investors will advise you to avoid these options. There are things you need to understand about the market before investing, but when you time the market well, they can work well and in your favour.

Since the year 2000 to date, I have worked on many multi-million pound development projects, which has allowed me to gain an in-depth knowledge of the property and property development sector.

I have always been interested in watching and following successful people. A few years ago, I decided to take a step back and take a look at the larger picture, which took me on a journey of personal development over the last few years. I have invested a lot of time and money in my own personal development, hiring mentors and training to become a world-class public speaker. I read that Warren Buffett considered public speaking to be a highly valued skill, which he had once feared himself, and invested in the best training to become good at public speaking. If you want to become successful, a good tip is to listen to the tips from those who are already successful, get a mentor and model their success.

Today, I continue to invest in property. I am now also building up a property investment and development training company to help others succeed in this area. I hope that you will be one of them and I will meet you at one of the events soon.

"The Best Investment That You Can Ever Make Is In Yourself, The Second-Best Investment That You Can Make Is In Property."
– Calum Kirkness

"Having Great Communication And Negotiation Skills Is One Of The Key Skills Required To Succeed In Property Investment, Property Development And Business."
– Calum Kirkness

"Model The Success Of People Who Have Already Reached The Level That You Would Like To Reach And Got There By A Means That You Would Be Happy To Model And Follow."
– Calum Kirkness

CHAPTER 2

WHY INVEST IN PROPERTY

Do you want to retire early and escape the rat race? Of course you do. This book is written to help you accomplish this goal and live the life of your dreams on your terms, which is within your reach regardless of your current situation today.

We would all like to have the freedom to do what we want, when we want, where we want and with who we want, and enjoy a comfortable retirement without worrying about money. Unfortunately, it is sad but true that a significantly large portion of the population will not have sufficient pension funds to support them in a comfortable retirement.

With the average life expectancy increasing, the period people are living in retirement is also increasing. This has resulted in increased pressure on the state pension, which is unlikely to be able to afford to support us all at the same level going forward. We are therefore likely to see further increases in the retirement age, and the erosion of the value of the pension payment. Most people will be unable to rely on their personal or company pension schemes to support them in retirement due to their level of performance, particularly over the last decade.

Have you ever taken the time to check and see how much your pension is currently worth? and what it is forecast to be worth at your retirement age? WARNING: it may shock you! Have you checked to see how much of your salary you would need to pay into a pension in order to retire with the same standard of living that you enjoy whilst working? WARNING: this may also shock you! If you haven't checked, it is worth doing. You can access free pension calculators online, where you put in different figures to see how much you would need to pay in each month to achieve a certain monthly pension amount in retirement.

The best way to ensure a comfortable retirement is to take control of your own destiny, which may be the reason that you are reading this book.

If you want to have financial freedom, a nice lifestyle and retire early and comfortably, you need to build a money-making machine, which harnesses the power of leverage and compounding to create a passive income stream for the rest of your lifetime. In other words, you must automate your savings and investments in a tax efficient manner that will continue to generate an income for you. The great thing about property is that you can use leverage and the power of the compound effect. We will look at leverage and compound effect throughout the book and how you can apply them in property investing.

> *"If You Want To Be Financially Free And Enjoy A Comfortable Retirement, You Need To Build A Money-Making Machine."*
> **— Calum Kirkness**

As I mentioned in the introduction, I have tried several different investment types and by far the best performer has always consistently been property by a large margin. Not only can property investment provide you with a comfortable retirement, it could allow you to retire early and live your dream lifestyle. Wouldn't that be a win-win?

Why Property Builds Wealth More Consistently Than Other Asset Class:

If you owned property during the most recent economic financial crash in 2008 and the following years of decline in property prices, or you followed the news and what was happening at the time, then the headlines might cause you some emotional pain. I personally remember the media headlines leading up to the peak and down to the trough. For some, I'm sure it felt like the market would never recover! Except for those living in, and around, London and Aberdeen at the time, where property prices continued to climb post 2008 and declined at different times later. More on microeconomics, and the reasons for this, later in the book.

Fast-forward a few years and prices throughout the rest of the country have slowly recovered, and people are building wealth through property again. The reason is, there was nothing fundamentally wrong with the market; the prices simply became unaffordable. Everyone was enjoying the party, which was being driven by the media, the banks and human behaviour, but like all good parties, they come to an end eventually and a hangover follows. The bigger and longer the party lasts, the bigger the hangover and the longer it takes to recover! During periods of recession, the rental sector tends to increase, and rents generally don't fall or not as fast as property values. This means that if you have bought well, and ensured the property cashflows well, you should be able to keep the property rented out during any recession and decline in property prices and come out the other end in pole position.

"The Bigger And Longer The Party Lasts, The Bigger The Hangover! Property Cycles Are The Same."
– Calum Kirkness

"Study And Prepare Whilst Others Are Busy Enjoying The Party, And Buy Whilst Others Are Suffering From The Hangover."
– Calum Kirkness

Those who were buying properties solely because prices were climbing, and for no other reason, only have one exit strategy: to sell later and hope that the property has increased in value. When the music stopped playing and the market stopped climbing, many of these so-called investors lost their shirts!

Wise investors purchase properties on a sound judgement that the property will generate more income than it costs to own during the period of ownership – known as cashflow. These investors who understand cashflow, and invest wisely, knowing that the cost of holding the property will be less than the ongoing rental income, are not so concerned about what the market values do. If prices drop, they know they are in a relatively safe position. If prices rise, they have more options. If we add "buying well" in to the equation and buying below market value (which we will cover in the book), then this further reduces any risk, accelerates the options, and speeds up the rate of growth in building your property investment portfolio.

One of the greatest forces on the value of an investment is supply and demand. Our supply of development land in the UK is limited, yet the population continues to increase. Everyone requires somewhere to live, so with property we have the force of supply and demand continuing to work in its favour.

The other great thing about property is the opportunity to use leverage on the amount of funds that you have available to invest, which is something that you cannot do with stocks.

And finally, not to forget the power of the compound effect, which is the most powerful of all once you understand it.

You may be thinking if property is such a good investment, why don't more people invest in it? Here are a few common reasons that prevent people from starting to invest in property or scale their property investment business and portfolio:

10 Things That Might Currently Be Holding You Back:

- **Lack of clarity** – You are not sure what you want to do or achieve, or you are confused from listening to others.
- **Lack of courage** – This is usually down to mindset, which we will look at later in the book.
- **Lack of knowledge** – A lot of people either don't know where to start to obtain the knowledge, think they require a lot of knowledge and don't bother to start, or some people never think they have enough knowledge and keep consuming more and more and never get started.
- **Lack of experience** – Experience is certainly valuable, but we all

have to start somewhere in order to get it. Having the right knowledge before starting reduces risk.

- **Lack of money** – This is a limiting belief and mindset issue, which we will look at later in the book. It is never the lack of resources that prevents people starting; it is the lack of resourcefulness that prevents them taking action.
- **Lack of time** – We all have the same amount of time each day, it's how we use it that matters.
- **Lack of patience** – Some things take time. Wealth is best built at a steady sustainable pace and we cover the reason why throughout the book. How many get rich schemes have you seen people succeed with? Not many, if any, I bet!
- **Lack of belief** – You don't believe in yourself or that you can achieve your goals. Pretty much anyone can become a successful property investor with the right knowledge and level of resourcefulness.
- **It seems like too much hard work** – The great thing about property investing is that you can use leverage and compound effect to ensure that your money is working for you, rather than you having to work for money. You can also outsource a lot of the tasks.

It is important to understand which of these factors may have been, or may currently be, limiting your progress and preventing you from taking action. Have a think about how much these beliefs may have cost you in missed opportunities to make serious amounts of money and build wealth.

Throughout the book, we will look at all these points in more detail and show you how to overcome them.

If you are not willing to learn, no one can help you. But if you are determined to learn, no one can stop you.

Be warned: this book goes deep. I would encourage you to read the book from cover to cover, without skipping any sections, and then read it again. You will see how each section links with the other and how each individual part is important in understanding the whole process. Missing just one or two key parts can have a massive impact on your overall results and success. It may be difficult and a bit uncomfortable to grasp the first time around, but once you have read the book a second time, the picture will become clearer and much easier to understand. The more you focus on a particular strategy and area, the easier and quicker you can build your expertise and success.

The opportunity for you to make serious amounts of money and build wealth from investing in property in the UK market is huge, it is real and the opportunities and possibilities are endless. It is available right now and it all begins with you raising your awareness and taking action on these ideas and information.

PROPERTY SUCCESS INSIDER FRAMEWORK 5F's &
PROPERTY SUCCESS INSIDER FORMULA 7P's

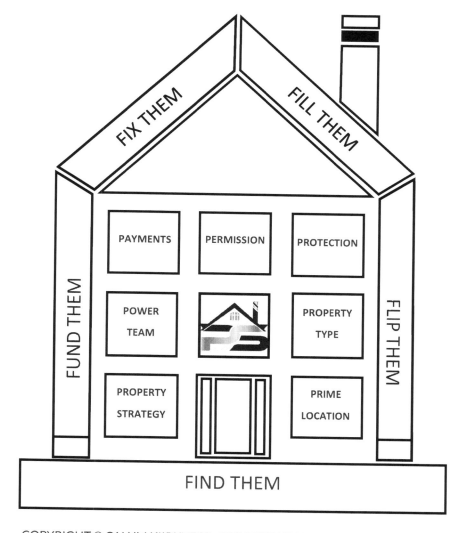

FIX THEM

FILL THEM

FUND THEM

FLIP THEM

PAYMENTS

PERMISSION

PROTECTION

POWER TEAM

PROPERTY TYPE

PROPERTY STRATEGY

PRIME LOCATION

FIND THEM

CHAPTER 3

PROPERTY STRATEGIES

The following chapter describes the basic principles of eight different property strategies. In the beginning, it is important to select the one that is right for you and focus on creating a niche where you become the go-to expert. You can always add other strategies when you become an expert in each one. As you go through the book, and particularly the next three chapters, the right strategy for you should begin to become apparent.

PROPERTY STRATEGY 1
BUY-TO-LET PROPERTY INVESTMENT STRATEGY

Source and buy good property.	Rent property six months plus on AST.	Hold forever or sell in the future.

What is Buy-to-Let?

Buy-to-let property investing is when a landlord purchases a property, which they then rent out as a single property to a tenant on an assured shorthold tenancy agreement. The minimum letting period is normally six months. Six or twelve months are the standard letting periods, and they can be renewed at the end of each agreed tenancy period on an ongoing basis. It is ideal to have good, long-stay tenants which helps reduce any void periods, as well as the marketing and work to find and secure new tenants.

Buy-to-let can be a great way to generate cashflow and have the potential to benefit from capital growth on the property over the long term. It works when you buy a suitable investment property in a good location and then prepare it for rental to a suitable tenant on an assured shorthold tenancy agreement.

I always recommend appointing a good letting agent to manage the property rather than self-managing it. A good letting agent will find a good tenant and carry out all the necessary paperwork to comply with all the statutory rules and regulations. It is important to follow all the correct procedures and ensure all the relevant paperwork is in place.

Why Invest In Buy-to-Let?

Due to low interest rates on savings in the bank and low returns in financial instruments such as ISA's and pension funds, people are seeing the value of their money depreciate or grow at a very slow pace, whilst the availability to access mortgages with low interest rates in recent years, has helped property deals stack up and added to the attraction of buy-to-let as a safe investment.

When considering buy-to-let in today's market, it is important to be aware of a few changes which have already affected, or are likely to affect the sector soon. The main changes are as follows:

- Low mortgage interest rates won't last forever and will rise. It is important to know that your investment will still stack up by doing a stress test. This means checking the numbers with a higher interest rate to see how much they can rise before your investment starts costing you more than the rent that you receive.
- The Government has introduced and put in place some tax changes on buy-to-let mortgage interest relief. The mortgage interest relief has been scrapped and replaced with a 20% tax credit. This affects higher tax rate payers, who have bought the property in their own name, quite significantly. There are possible alternatives to reduce the impact. More on this later in the book.

- The Government has also introduced an additional tax where landlords must pay an additional 3% stamp duty on investment property purchases. It is important to get expert advice, as there are circumstances when the additional 3% stamp duty may not be applicable. There is a stamp duty calculator available at: https://www.stampdutycalculator.org.uk/ It is advisable to get expert advice from a property tax specialist.
- It is also worth noting that the Bank of England has buy-to-let mortgages in its sights and is likely to impose some changes.

Despite these tax changes and the potential for buy-to-let mortgage costs to rise, there are still positives in the buy-to-let sector:

- The changes have led to a number of landlords selling part, or all, of their property portfolios, which has reduced the number of available rental properties.
- The changes have led to a number of existing landlords, particularly those in the higher tax bracket and want to keep their properties, changing their strategy to Houses of Multiple Occupancy (HMO) and Serviced Accommodation (SA), which has led to a decline in the number of BTL rental properties being available.
- The demand for rental properties continues to rise.
- Due to the change in balance between supply and demand, rental prices have increased.
- The Government have their sights on landlords and there are likely to be further measures imposed on the sector, possibly rent controls. I think this will just lead to more people switching strategy or selling up, creating an even greater imbalance in supply and demand in the BTL sector.

Whilst these changes may sound all doom and gloom, once you understand the fundamentals of the property market and how things work, which we go into more detail throughout the book, it could indicate that these may be good conditions for the smart investors to capitalise on an opportunity.

Like any investment, buy-to-let comes with no guarantees, but for those who have more faith in bricks and mortar than stocks and shares, it can be a great investment vehicle and money-making machine.

Before investing, there are several key things that you need to know and follow:

- Research the buy-to-let market.
- Research and select a good, or promising, location to invest in.
- Research suitable properties.
- Do your due diligence, including the numbers.
- Get the best buy-to-let mortgage.
- Think about your ideal tenant.
- Negotiate the best price when investing in property.
- Know the pitfalls of buy-to-let.
- Consider how hands-on a landlord you want to be.

Once you buy a property, you can potentially earn a profit in two ways:

- **Cashflow** – this is the difference between income that your tenant(s) pays you in rent, minus all expenditure costs such as mortgage payments, maintenance, insurance, repairs and agents' fees, etc. It should always be a positive figure.
- **Capital growth and gain** – if you buy well in a good location, you should see the value of your investment property increase over time. The capital gain is the profit you achieve when you sell your property for more than you paid for it. You can also access the gain by re-mortgaging the property to release the equity to purchase more properties.

Let's have a look at an example deal for illustration purposes.

You should always aim to buy below market value (BMV) and make money when you buy property.

BMV BTL Deal Calculations		
Market value		£100,000
Purchase price		£75,000
Below market value discount amount		£25,000
Below market value discount %	25.00	
((PV-PP)/PV) x100		
BTL Mortgage 75% of purchase price		£56,250
Mortgage arrangement fee added to mortgage		£995
Mortgage amount including fee		£57,245
Mortgage interest rate 4%	4.00	
Deposit 25% of purchase price	25	£18,750
Property offers an annual gross rental yield of 7%	7.00	£7,000.00
Monthly rental (£7,000 / 12 months)		£583.33
Monthly Cashflow Calculations		
Description	Income	Expenditure
Monthly rental	£583.33	
Mortgage payment per month (£57,245 x 4%)		£190.82
Letting agent fee – 10% of rent		£58.33
Insurance		£20.00
Repairs allowance – 10% of rent		£58.33
Total Income and Outgoings	£583.33	£327.48
Monthly Cashflow = Income – Expenditure		£255.85
Annual Passive Income		£3,070.20

Some investors like to know what their return on investment is in relation to the money that they have invested. Let's take a look at how this is calculated.

Return on Investment based on cashflow only	
Funds Invested	**Amount**
Deposit 25% purchase price	£18,750
Stamp duty 3% £75,000	£2,250
Legal costs	£800
Surveys and fees	£700
Renovation costs	£3,000
Total Initial Investment	**£25,500**
Return on investment based on annual cashflow of £3,070.20) as a % of own funds invested	12.05

Most people would consider 12.05% return on their money invested to be a good return.

The good news is that it can get even better if we factor in potential future capital growth. Based on history, provided you have bought in a good location, the property is likely to go up in value over time. Let's have a look at how capital growth can benefit.

Capital Growth	
Market value of the property	£100,000
Increase in market value @ 6% annually	£6,000

So, in year one with a 6% increase in the value of the property, your wealth has increased by an additional £6,000. If we now add capital growth in year one to the annual cashflow amount, this gives us the total potential year one gain from the deal as follows.

Year One: Cashflow + Capital Growth	
Annual cashflow	£3,070
Annual capital growth	£6,000
Total cashflow and capital growth	**£9,070**

Now let's have a look at the return on investment based on cashflow and capital growth added together.

Initial Funds Invested	Amount
Total initial funds investment	£25,500
Annual gain from cashflow and capital growth in year one	£9,070
% Return on investment based own funds invested	**35.57**

I am sure most people would consider a 35.57% return on investment to be an excellent result.

Let's now take it a stage further and get the original funds invested in the deal back out as quickly as possible, and look at the results.

Mortgage rules are such that in most circumstances it is not possible to re-mortgage a property for at least six months. Given that the property was purchased below market value, it means that there is equity sitting in the deal that could be accessed via re-mortgage and used to help fund the next deal.

For the example, we will assume that the £3,000 renovation to the property has added £5,000 to the value and the property has increased in value by 3% over the first six months of ownership.

BTL Re-mortgage at MV to Release Equity Calculation		
Market value		£108,000
BTL mortgage 75% market value	75	£81,000
Less previous mortgage balance		£57,245
Balance of funds released from re-mortgage		**£23,755**

From the calculation above, we can see that the investor could access £23,755 equity in the deal by re-mortgaging the property after six months. If the investor decided to do this and use the funds to repay themselves, the investor would only have a small amount of their original investment still left in the deal, which equals (£25,500 - £23,755) = £1,745.

When re-mortgaging, it is important to consider the impact the higher mortgage amount will have on the cashflow.

BTL Cashflow Calculations after Re-mortgaging		
Market value		£100,000
Purchase price		£75,000
Below market value discount amount		£25,000
Below market value discount %	25.00	
((PV-PP)/PV) x100		
New BTL mortgage 75% market value	75	£75,000
Mortgage arrangement fee added to mortgage		£995
Mortgage amount including fee		**£75,995**
Mortgage interest rate 4%	4.00	
Original deposit 25%	25	£18,750
Property offers a gross rental yield of 7%	7.00	£7,000.00
Monthly rental (£7,000 / 12 months)		£583.33
Monthly Cashflow Calculations		
Description	**Income**	**Expenditure**
Monthly rental	£583.33	
Mortgage payment per month (£75,995 x 4%)/12		**£253.32**
Letting agent 10% of rent		£58.33
Insurance		£20.00
Repairs allowance 10% of rent		£58.33
Total Income and Outgoings	**£583.33**	**£389.98**
Monthly Cashflow = Income - Expenditure		**£193.35**
Annual Passive Income		**£2,320.20**

Based on the above, we can still see that the property is still producing a positive cashflow of £193.35 per month based on the higher mortgage amount.

Given that the investor only has £1,745 of their original funds left in the deal after re-mortgaging, and they have had six months positive cashflow of £255.85 = £1,535.10, they only have (£1,745 - £1,535.10) = £209.10 left in the deal. If we then divide £209.10 by £193.35 being the new monthly cashflow amount to calculate how long it would take to have no money left in the deal, which = just over one month. In this example, the investor can have all their initial funds back out in seven to eight months and still enjoy an ongoing monthly cashflow and potential capital growth for however long they hold the property, which is an infinite return on investment.

From this example, we can see the benefit and the power of leverage by using an interest-only BTL mortgage and buying the property below market value.

If your investment criteria are not as ambitious and strict as the above example, and you are prepared to invest with an initial lower discount to market value at the time of purchase and take longer to get your funds back out, property can still make an excellent investment. It all depends on your goals, how quickly you want to achieve them, your level of risk and your level of commitment. These factors are covered in more detail throughout the book.

You can achieve the same effect as buying below market value by adding value to the property. Where the cost of the works being carried out is less than the value being added to the property. By doing this you create equity, which you can then access via re-mortgaging the property later. Where you see the potential to add a lot of value to a property, it means that you can consider paying the market value to purchase it. You want to make money when you a buy property though, so as an investor it would be rare to pay market value for a property.

If you can buy a property BMV that you can also add value to with a BTL mortgage, you have three means of leverage working in your favour.

BTL Should Be Viewed As A Long-Term Buy And Hold Strategy

Provided you buy the right property in the right location, there are benefits to holding the property long term and benefitting from capital growth and the compound effect. Every property that you add to your BTL portfolio should be bringing you additional cashflow each month, as well as the potential for capital growth. I believe the best way to create long-term wealth is to hold on to your property assets long term, even through the downturns. It costs time and money to sell and re-buy properties, which can be equal to a large part of the drop in values; you lose out on the rental income during the process and have to go through the process of buying again once the recession and fall in property values has bottomed out. More on this later.

10 Benefits Of Holding Properties In Your Portfolio Long Term Or Forever:

1. You continue to earn an income on the properties for life.
2. The income can be passive, providing you have a good letting agent in place.
3. Your money is now working for you, rather than the other way around.
4. If you are investing as an individual, you can access lumps of tax-free cash through re-mortgaging as the property increases in value, and not pay tax on the equity released.
5. No capital gains tax to pay, provided you never sell the property.
6. You can retire on the income, and even retire early, if you hit your targets earlier than retirement age, which is possible. If you require funds, you can always sell off one of your worst-performing properties.
7. The process can be systemised and is easily repeated.
8. The model is predictable and solid through market changes.
9. Your income and capital growth compound year on year as you build up your portfolio.
10. It gives you greater flexibility than a pension scheme, where you

can retire early if you wish, provided you have bought and managed the properties well.

The longer you own the property or properties, the more powerful the strategy becomes, provided you haven't bought a pig in a poke, in which case it is best to take the lesson and get rid of it without delay and move on.

I meet a lot of people who wish they hadn't sold their house 10, 20, 30 years ago, myself included. Here are some figures to demonstrate:

I sold a house back in 2000 (The one I referred to earlier in the book that the farmer bought) for £85,000, which recently sold for £225,000. Like the land that it sits on, most of that capital appreciation happened between 2000 and 2008.

What Are The Risks Of Buy-To-Let Investing?

- **Monthly Rental Amount** – rents can vary depending on market conditions but tend to be more stable than property prices in a downturn. Rents tend to increase over time but it is important to note that rents are not guaranteed.
- **Void Periods** – If you can't find tenants, you will have to cover all the expenses and mortgage repayments during the void period. It is better to keep the rental rates for the property competitive and have long-term happy tenants, than going for top of the market rental prices and tenants moving at the end of their tenancy agreement.
- **Property Prices Drop** – the value of property can go down as well as up, which might mean that you are not able to sell it for as much as you hoped. If you plan to keep the property long term and the property is cash flowing well, it can be better to hold the property long term. If you must sell and the sale price doesn't cover the whole mortgage (known as negative equity), you will be liable to make up the difference.
- **Difficult Tenants** – late or non-payment tenants can lead to increased costs and unexpected problems.

- **Interest Rate Increase** – depending on the type of mortgage that you have on the property, the monthly interest amount can increase if interest rates go up. It is important to stress test an increase in interest rates when doing your due diligence and calculations, and assess the risk.
- **Major Repairs** – things like boiler breakdowns can come as a surprise and take you out of the game if you do not have a contingency fund set aside. It is always advisable to set aside at least 10% of the rental income for maintenance and repairs.

Are Buy-To-Let Property Investments Safe And Secure?

Property is generally seen as one of the safest investments that you can make. Like all investments though, there are no guarantees and it is important to protect the downside and have insurance in place where appropriate.

- **Landlord insurance** – This isn't a legal requirement, but taking out a policy can help protect you and your investment and it is recommended.
- **Landlord buildings insurance** – This is required if you have a buy-to-let mortgage. Regardless if you have a mortgage on the property or not, it is advisable to protect your investment.
- **Landlord contents insurance** – This isn't a legal requirement, but is advisable depending on the level to which you furnish the property.

Once you know how the strategy works for one BTL property, it is relatively easy to develop a replicable system for buying further single buy-to-let properties with an average discount of 10-25% and a net yield of 2%+.

Depending on your end goal and the value of the properties that you invest in, this will determine how many properties you will need to meet your goals. You might need 10-20 to replace your current earned income, or you might need 30-40 properties to be totally financially independent.

Where To Source Buy-To-Let Opportunities

There are many ways to source properties which are suitable for BTL. The main methods are through estate agents and the online property portals. You could consider trying your luck at auction, but the best way is to source direct from the vendor. Knowing what to look for in a BTL is vital, and successful investors will know instantly whether a deal is suitable for BTL or not. Always do your own due diligence and do not take any values that an estate agent, sourcer or vendor will tell you as being accurate.

What should you be looking for?

The ideal property depends on the following factors:

- The type of property – BTL can work with most property types from flats to terraced and detached properties.
- The size of property – BTL tends to work best with one to three-bed properties.
- The condition of the property – This will depend on your strategy and how much work you are willing to do to bring the property up to a good walk-in liveable standard. If you are looking to add value, buying a property that requires work can be a good strategy.
- The location of the property – Location is important: tenants look for convenience and a good location will tend to appeal to them and increase the potential for capital growth over the long term.
- The value of the property – This will depend on the area where you are investing. Avoid the top and bottom ends of the market.
- The level of works required to create an attractive walk-in property – It is important to consider the cost of the works and the time it will take to complete them. Whilst the works are being carried out, you lose out on potential income and also have the costs of holding the property.

Advantages of BTL:

- One of the easiest and most straightforward strategies to understand.
- Ideal if you have funds to invest and cover the deposit/buying costs on your first investment property.
- Long-term investment and capital growth.
- Lower cashflow, but generally steady as tenants tend to stay longer than with an HMO.
- Passive income, particularly if using a letting agent to manage the property.
- Easy to manage.
- Only one set of tenants to deal with.
- Low maintenance with the right tenants.
- Doesn't take up much time.
- Less wear and tear than HMO and SA (serviced accommodation).
- Can re-mortgage property and release any equity in the future as the value of the property increases.
- Relatively easy to find good quality letting agents/property managers.

Disadvantages of BTL:

- Not suitable for rent-to-rent model: cashflow is too low.
- Lower rental income than some of the higher cashflow strategies.
- Void periods mean total loss of income until a new tenant is found.
- Need 25% deposit to purchase property, plus buying costs.
- Value of property can go down as well as up.
- It can take time and be difficult to get rid of bad tenants. Ensure you dot the i's and cross the t's at time of letting.
- Time and cost to sell property.
- Due to the recent government tax changes, in relation to how mortgage interest is calculated and offset against income, the BTL strategy may not be suitable for higher rate tax payers to own the properties in their own name. There is an option to purchase the

properties through a limited company. It is important to speak to an accountant and tax advisor who specialise in property to get advice on the best route to take.

Based on the investment factors covered throughout this book. I believe that the buy-to-let sector will remain a sound investment strategy.

PROPERTY STRATEGY 2
BUY-TO-FLIP (BUY-TO-SELL)

| Source and buy suitable properties. | Add value by refurbishment/ renovation/ extending. | Sell on completion. |

Buy-to-flip is a good strategy If you are looking for large lump sums of cash in a shorter period of time, or larger scale projects where you want maximum return on your time invested.

Buying to flip is about buying a property with the intention to add value to it and sell it on as quickly as possible for a profit. The viability of the strategy largely depends on the ability to buy the property at the right price for the market conditions at the time. For example, it is much easier to flip a property in a growing market, but also harder to get the properties at the right price during these times. With the right knowledge and experience, professionals can successfully flip property at any time during the property cycle.

Due to the buying and selling costs of a property, successful buy-to-flip relies on good negotiation and speed of execution. The faster an investor can flip the property, the lower the holding costs they will need to pay for items such as interest and finance charges, property taxes, utilities, etc.

Buy-to-flip investors generally follow the 70% rule. For example, if a property would be worth £100,000 in walk-in condition but needs £20,000 of renovation to bring it up to that value, an investor will purchase the home for £50,000 ((£100,000 x 70%) – (£20,000)) and seek to sell it for the full £100,000 when completed.

Buy-to-flip is a popular, and ideal, strategy with builders and tradespeople as they already have a lot of the skills required and trade accounts to buy the materials at competitive prices. However, this does not guarantee them success, and many tradespeople are unable to succeed with the strategy for reasons which will become apparent as you go through the book. Buy-to-flip has also become popular with the ambitious amateur property investor, due to the number of television programmes showing people the strategy in 30 minutes, which makes it look easy! Or easier than it is in reality!

Buy-to-flip is a property trading strategy rather than a property investment strategy and is therefore classed by the HMRC as a business. You are required to register your business with HMRC as a sole trader, partnership, LLP or Limited Company.

In order to decide which business structure will be the best for you, it is advisable to speak to an accountant and tax advisor who specialise in property, to advise you on the best and most tax-efficient structure for your unique circumstances and goals. When you work hard to make money and build wealth, it is important to think smart and hold on to as much of it as possible.

Adding value to property via refurbishment, renovation or extensions is great if you enjoy being hands-on. It can teach you many valuable and transferable skills such as: building skills and knowledge, procurement of materials and contractors, project management, cost and money management, communication, negotiation, and building your power team, etc. If you enjoy this part of the work, once you have the knowledge and experience, you can start offering a project management service to other investors.

A common mistake that newbies make is thinking that a quick coat of paint and decoration will add thousands of pounds of value to an otherwise decent property. If the only work required to the property is redecoration, then it is not something that an experienced trader would consider buying unless they were able to secure the property with a substantial discount.

What should you be looking for?

The ideal property depends on the following factors:

- The type of property.
- The size of property.
- The condition of the property.
- The location of the property.
- The value of the property.
- The level of work required to create an attractive walk-in property.
- Demand in the area.

If you are new to flipping property, then it is best to start with smaller properties in a lower price bracket requiring light refurbishment first. You may not make as much profit, but you will gain valuable knowledge, experience and skills, which you can carry forward and scale to future projects.

Refurbishment, renovation, reconfiguration and extension of property can be broken down into four levels, starting with the easiest level and working up to the hardest as follows:

Refurbishment:

- Light refurbishment.
- Medium level refurbishment.
- Major refurbishment.

Renovation:

- Light renovation.
- Medium level renovation.
- Major renovation.

Reconfiguration:

- Small reconfiguration – Changing layout slightly.

- Medium reconfiguration – Changing layout to create additional bedrooms.
- Major reconfiguration – Largely changing internal layout.

Extension:

- Small extension or loft conversion.
- Medium level extension.
- Major extension.

One of the great things about buy-to-flip is that it is a highly leverageable strategy. Successful property flippers typically have several projects on the go at the same time. For this to be successful, it requires excellent project and cost management skills to ensure that you have the right materials on-site, in time for the right people to be doing the right tasks, at the right time and at the right price. It is essential to ensure that the increase in the selling price justifies the work that is being carried out.

Adding value to the property to make a profit on the flip can be achieved by:

- Buying at a discount and adding further value through refurbishment.
- Buying at market value and spotting the potential to add value through refurbishment, renovation, reconfiguration, adding an extension, title splitting or converting a loft, garage, basement, etc.

The type of works to add value to the property should be considered with the next owner in mind. Newbies typically make the mistake of allowing their own tastes and emotions to get involved, resulting in the wrong type of work being carried out, and creating the wrong property, in the wrong area, for the wrong potential buyer.

The position and location of the property will largely dictate what type of potential buyers the upgraded property will attract. It is important to research the area and understand the type of buyer the property is likely to attract, and then carry out the works accordingly. This will ensure the best selling price and reduce the time it takes to sell the property, which in turn reduces finance costs and increased profit. Time = Money.

One of the challenges with the buy-to-flip strategy is accurately understanding the costs of the work required to add value to the property. This is a fundamental piece of the jigsaw, which many people do not understand and get wrong. It is fundamental to understand what the property value will be once the works have been carried out, and how much the cost of the work and the buying costs will be in order to determine the maximum price that you can pay for the property in the first place.

Profit Potential

It is important to know, and set, your property investment criteria and goals before you start. Think about the minimum profit that you would want to make from a buy-to-flip and then work back from there.

Key factors to include when determining whether a deal stacks up or not:

- Knowing what the likely end sale price of the property is. A great tool to use when starting out is the 'Sold Prices' tab on Rightmove.co.uk. This tool will tell you how much other properties in the area sold for. Make your comparison based on as close a like-for-like basis as possible.
- Know the cost of the works to upgrade and add value to the property. Include a contingency sum.
- Know the costs of finance to fund the deal.
- Know the buying and selling costs.
- Know your investment criteria for profit level, or % based on project value or funds invested.
- Know how long the project is likely to take from completion of purchase to completion of sale.
- Once you know all the above, you can calculate the maximum purchase price that you can pay for the property.

Example Buy to Flip Deal Calculation	
Purchase price	£50,000
Cost of works to add value	£18,000
Contingency on cost of works @ 10%	£2,000
Buying costs	£3,000
Funding costs	£4,000
Selling costs	£3,000
Total projected costs	**£80,000**
Projected end value	**£100,000**
Profit = Difference between total costs and projected end value / sale price	**£20,000**
Profit margin as a % of GDV	**20%**

If your investment criteria were to make 20% profit on the sale price, then this deal would stack up. If the profit was less than your investment criteria, you would need to negotiate a reduction in the purchase price, or find more cost-efficient ways of carrying out the works.

It Is Always Advisable to Have a Favourable Second Exit Strategy Option

I always like to have two exit strategies that stack up when going into any deal. For example, if the property failed to sell when it was finished. If you have done your due diligence and know that the deal also stacks up for buy-to-let, then you have massively reduced the risk of the deal and can enjoy some cashflow from the rental income and sell the property later. It is important to understand that good buy-to-flip areas are not the best buy-to-let areas, but it doesn't mean to say that a property wouldn't rent in the area, just that the yield may be lower than a good buy-to-let area.

Where to Source Buy-To-Flip Opportunities

There are many ways to source properties which are suitable to be flipped. The main one is through estate agents, but the best way is to source direct to vendor. Knowing what to look for in a buy-to-flip is vital, and successful traders will know instantly whether a deal is suitable for flipping or not.

Always do your own due diligence and do not take any values that an estate agent, sourcer or vendor will tell you as being accurate.

Some Advantages Of Flipping:

- The main advantage is the ability to make a larger sum of profit in a short period of time, and use the capital for your next investment.
- Property markets tend to be stable, which allows you to develop realistic financial projections.
- Flipping means your capital is at risk for a shorter period of time.
- There are no rental agreements and therefore no tenant risks.

50 Buy-To-Flip Tips:

1. Always start with the end in mind. Know your buyer type, the demand for properties in the area and the projected property value when the project is complete.
2. The easiest and best properties to flip are two- to three-bed terraced, semi-detached and detached houses in good locations, which are also good projects to start on.
3. Start with small, easy projects and work your way up as you gain more knowledge, experience, and build and strengthen your power team.
4. Make sure you have the correct project finance in place on the right terms. Watch out for redemption penalties.
5. Do your due diligence and stick to your investment criteria. The numbers don't lie.
6. Don't get emotional about the house; it's all about the numbers and end buyer.
7. You make your money when you buy, not when you sell. You need to do your due diligence to ensure you are paying the correct price to make the deal work.
8. Buy the worst properties in the best locations that you can afford: location is key.
9. Ideally invest in buy-to-flip property close to where you live to cut down on travel time and costs.

10. Find something to set yourself apart from the rest of the developers. Don't be afraid to stand out.

11. Expect to submit a lot of offers before you get a deal. Persistence and consistency are the key.

12. If you're not embarrassed with your first offer, then it's not low enough!

13. Justify your offer – list all the costs to renovate the property and remember to include all buying and selling costs.

14. Include transactional and holding costs, such as solicitors' fees for both buying and selling, agent fees, finance, planning permission, building control fees, insurance, utility bills, searches, surveys, structural engineer fees (if applicable), etc.

15. Invite several local estate agents round and ask them what they would recommend that you do to secure the best price. They are the experts on selling who know the buyer demand.

16. Be careful not to over or under spec your project. Always have your end purchasers' desires in mind.

17. It is important to keep up to date with the current market situation and understand the strategies that are working at the time. What worked two years ago, or even last year, may not work now or in the future.

18. Depending on your level of buy-to-flip knowledge and experience, you should consider getting a good builder and project manager to run the project for you. People management skills and understanding scheduling and sequencing are vital for the success of buy-to-flip projects.

19. Closely monitor your project manager to learn further knowledge on the process, which you can carry forward and use on future projects.

20. Always be planning ahead: lack of information and changes during the project will lead to delays, increased costs and possibly losing some key tradespeople.

21. Stick to local trades where possible so that you don't get hit with hidden travel and fuel charges.

22. Put together a detailed schedule of works, and only pay when each agreed phase has been completed to your satisfaction.
23. Write out an itemised specification for your builder.
24. Create timelines and stick to them: time is money when flipping.
25. Kitchen and bathrooms are important. Refurb to the standard of the asking price; these can make or break a project. If they don't appeal to buyers, they know that these items are expensive and disruptive to replace.
26. Skillful delegation is vital in any business.
27. Source as much of the materials yourself and try to buy through the trade accounts of friends or contacts.
28. Get at least three quotes for everything.
29. Get everything in writing and agreed upfront with your builder.
30. On your first few projects visit the site daily to maximise the learning, and at least twice per week to monitor progress and deal with any issues as they arise once you have more knowledge and experience.
31. Projects can and regularly run over time and budget. Include a contingency of 10-20% for both time and costs when working out your overall costs.
32. Always get references from your builder and speak to their past and present customers, and visit some of their projects.
33. Associate with investors who are already doing what you aspire to do. They will hold you accountable and will become a valuable resource.
34. Get professional advice.
35. Always meet the planning officer and build rapport with them. Some can be very helpful and may offer you more flexibility.
36. People buy from those they know, like and trust; aim to get all three qualities in your builder and project team.
37. Make yourself easy to work with by paying on time but never in advance. Payment in advance removes all motivation to get the work done!
38. Allow plenty of time and money in the budget for the finish. This is

what the buyer sees and what they base their buying decision on.

39. Provide visually appealing and quality fixtures, fittings and décor. This is what the people see.

40. In order to achieve top price, a buyer must fall in love with the property. Include at least one WOW factor, but don't go overboard.

41. Never try to cut costs by doing your own painting and decorating unless you are a professional. This is the finish that people see.

42. Keep décor as neutral as possible.

43. Appearances and first impressions matter. Make sure the front of the property is appealing to passersby. You don't get a second chance to make a first impression.

44. Use the building phase to install nice hoarding that brands your company and name in the area. Make it professional in appearance and keep the site tidy.

45. Always take before and after photographs, as well as progress photos. They are good to look back on, good for records of electrics and plumbing, etc., and also good for proof should you need it. Use them with vendors or agents to show your experience and you can use them for marketing purposes as well.

46. Consider having the property staged by a professional company if it hasn't already sold by the time it is complete.

47. Be open and prepared to accept an offer. Attempting to hold out for just a little more can be a mistake and false economy, which often costs more in holding costs than the difference between the asking and offer price. Remember: Time = Money.

48. Good property rental areas are not the same as good flipping areas. Each has a different set of criteria.

49. Education is the key. Remember: you don't know what you don't know.

50. Have a good mentor to guide you through the process and support you when things don't go to plan.

You can find more helpful information about flipping a property in the Property Development Section, which is a more advanced strategy than buy-to-flip.

PROPERTY STRATEGY 3
HOUSE MULTIPLE OCCUPATION (HMO)

Source and buy / control property.	Rent property per room – normally for period of six months plus on AST.	If own property, hold forever or sell at a later date. If property is controlled via Rent-to-Rent Agreement, hold property for period of R2R Agreement and renew or allow agreement to expire.

HMO is a relatively new strategy and generally considered one of the new accelerated cashflow strategies. The demand for the HMO strategy has grown fast in the last decade, particularly in larger towns and cities due to several factors:

- **Affordability** – People cannot afford to buy property like they used to due to affordability and property prices. They also cannot afford to rent whole properties for themselves due to property rental prices.
- **Population growth** is increasing. Towns and cities are becoming more and more densely populated without the available land to build more properties on.
- **Developer margins** – It has become harder and harder for developers to make the profit margins that they look for, so they build smaller and smaller houses and flats to reduce costs.

- **Careers are more transient** and people do not hold down jobs, or relationships, for as long as they used to. This means they need more flexible living accommodation to match their changing lifestyles.
- **Government changes** – Recently introduced Government changes to mortgage interest tax relief has resulted in some property investors changing strategy to minimise or eliminate the negative financial implications of the tax change.

You may have noticed many large houses, nursing homes and commercial and office buildings have been converted into HMO multi-let room properties.

HMO can be operated from property that you own or from property that you control via a rent-to-rent agreement. An HMO can be a great and relatively easy strategy to get started in property.

How Does The HMO Strategy Work?

- **Set up your business structure** in consultation with your specialist property accountant and tax advisor.
- **Select your prime location and goldmine area** to operate your HMO properties in. It is important that you understand the area you are looking to operate an HMO in and what type of people it attracts. Check with the local authority regarding any restrictions and licensing requirements.
- **Find a suitable property** – An HMO can be operated from property that you own or property that you control under some form of lease agreement. HMOs generally work best on properties with at least four or more bedrooms, and the living room is used as an additional bedroom making five lettable rooms. The rooms are let on an individual basis, which results in a higher rental income from the property than letting it as one complete property. It is important to note that there are also higher expenses and more time involved in operating an HMO compared to buy-to-let. It is important to check with the local authority where the property is

to understand their rules and regulations before offering on a property.

- **Make an offer to purchase or rent the property** if you do not already own it, and set out the benefits to the property owner of choosing you.

- **Set up the property** – There are a number of rules and regulations affecting HMOs, which are on the increase. It is important that you keep up to date with these changes in order to be compliant. It is also important to note that the Government and local authority regulations can differ. It is always best to speak to your local HMO Officer, and carry out any works required to the property in order to comply with the local rules and regulations. The property should be furnished to a standard that would be expected from your ideal tenant. Make sure the utilities are set up and don't forget the crucial broadband!

- **Self-manage or appoint an agent** – Decide if you are going to manage the property yourself or appoint a letting agent to manage the property for you. It is not easy to find a good agent to manage HMO properties and I would advise managing these yourself if you cannot find a good agent.

- **Find suitable tenants** – It is important to understand what type of tenant you wish to attract and provide accommodation for. There are five different types of tenants:

    o **High-end** – This model provides hotel room-like accommodation for high-end professionals in or near affluent parts of towns or cities, therefore attracting the best tenants and commanding the highest room rental rates. In order to attract high-end tenants, the property needs to be furnished accordingly, which requires the largest initial investment. Providing it is set up and run well, it is the most profitable HMO model.

    o **Professional/Young professionals** – This model offers a slightly larger market, with less input costs for you or your JV partner.

- ○ **Blue collar** – This offers a larger market than professional, and it is not as necessary to be right in the town centre where prices are often higher, as these can be located close to the main industry of the town/city, for example, near the hospital or a large manufacturing plant. There is less input cost. Tenants are less fussy about the quality of the accommodation and perhaps an extra room can be squeezed in per house. The lower down the 5-step model you go, the more management the tenants are likely to need.

- ○ **Students** – This model is especially effective in University towns and cities, especially where the property is located within one mile of campus and has good access to public transport. Vacant periods are higher because of long holiday periods, and maintenance and management are also higher, but tenant expectations are lower and there is a greater tolerance of higher numbers. Accordingly, rent is set higher.

- ○ **LHA/DSS** – This segment offers the lowest amount of capital outlay to start, but also commands the lowest rent per room and requires the highest management in terms of time and costs. Space can be maximised to great effect. The tenant turnover can be high.

Repeat and scale what works until you reach your financial and lifestyle goals.

When operating an HMO, the landlord or operator normally receives a deposit and lump sum monthly rental payment from the tenant, and the landlord covers all the utility costs, council tax maintenance, etc.

Example:

A four-bedroom property with one living room is on a rent-to-rent agreement in your goldmine area. As a single-let property, the landlord can expect to receive £1,000 per month.

You have researched your goldmine area and there is high demand for rooms in the area and no restriction on operating HMOs, so registration and licencing should be straightforward. You have assessed that individual rooms in the area will rent for £450 per month, giving a total monthly income of £2,200 (five bedrooms x £450 per month).

As described above, with HMO properties the landlord/operator covers all the expenses.

An HMO property has higher regulations and you will be required to bring the property up to the standards required, such as fire regulations, etc. which will have an upfront cost.

The landlord will also be required to provide a basic furniture package in each room and provide appliances and equipment in the kitchen.

HMO Cashflow Calculations	Income	Expenditure
Income (5 bedrooms x £450 per room per month)	£2,200	
Expenditure		
Monthly rent to property owner		£1,000
Council Tax		£150
Utility bills		£250
Broadband		£50
Insurance		£50
Maintenance/wear and tear 10%		£220
Licences		£20
Marketing costs		£50
Total income and expenditure	**£2,200**	**£1,790**
Monthly profit at 100% occupancy	**£410**	

You can see from this example, that the profit/cashflow from an HMO is not much more than a single buy-to-let once all costs are taken in to consideration. HMO properties also take more time, effort and hassle to operate than single buy-to-let properties.

Some Advantages Of An HMO:

- Suitable for property that you own or via rent-to-rent agreement
- Rent-to-rent offers lower initial costs than buying a property.
- Rental yields can be higher than single buy-to-let.
- Void periods cause less damage to your rental income. Given that there are multiple separate tenants it is unlikely, although not impossible, that the property is completely empty.
- The demand for property continues to rise in the UK, especially from young people, so the demand for HMO rooms is likely to increase.

Some Disadvantages Of An HMO:

- HMO properties are heavily regulated and becoming increasingly more so.
- HMO properties need a license to operate. There are rules which govern HMO licensing, although each local authority has their own specific set of rules on the exact details. It is important to check with the local authority where the HMO is and not get caught out by any differences between government and local authority regulations.
- The costs of converting an HMO can be high, particularly when the property is not well-suited for conversion.
- There are extra requirements for fire safety, etc. which need to be complied with.
- Tenant turnover can often be high, which means a lot of extra work and costs in advertising, marketing and vetting new tenants.
- HMO is not a passive income unless you can find a good letting agent who can manage your HMO well, which is very hard to find. Or you systemise and scale your HMO business and employ your own team.
- HMO involves dealing with a lot more people than a traditional buy-to-let.
- HMO has a lot more moving parts and things can and regularly go wrong.

- HMO often involves complete strangers sharing a property together, which can lead to problems.
- HMO finance can be harder to obtain, and the mortgage interest rate tends to be higher.
- HMOs can be harder to sell.

I am sure HMO is a strategy that is here for the long term due to lack of supply and affordability of housing, and I am sure that there will be some people who will do very well from this strategy in the coming years.

PROPERTY STRATEGY 4
SERVICED ACCOMMODATION (SA)

Source good properties – buy / control property.	Rent property per night / week up to one month.	If own property, hold forever or sell at a later date. If property is controlled via Rent-to-Rent Agreement, hold property for period of R2R Agreement and renew or allow agreement to expire.

What is Serviced Accommodation?

Serviced accommodation is taking normal apartments and houses and preparing them for guests to rent on a nightly basis for up to a period of one month. SA is like operating an unmanned hotel, with no staff, no bar and no restaurant. The critical difference between serviced accommodation and a standard buy-to-let or HMO property is that instead of renting the property using a six-month assured short-hold tenancy agreement (AST), the property is rented out on a nightly basis for up to one month to the guest(s). You should never rent the property to the same guest continuously for a period of more than one month as it could run the risk of being classified as their main residence, which creates an AST and their status changes from guest to tenant.

There are many moving parts to a serviced accommodation, which makes it a strategy which is more challenging to set up and operate than some of the other property strategies. There is a process that needs to be followed to set up and operate a successful serviced accommodation property. For starters, you need to have the appropriate business structure set up, you need to have all the relevant consents and planning permission in place, the correct finance, the correct insurance and that is just for starters. Then, there is the marketing and operational systems to set up. There is a lot of paperwork involved in operating a serviced accommodation business, but it can be a very rewarding strategy if set up and operated well. It is ideal if you are a people person and enjoy serving others.

Like all property strategies, there are different types of serviced accommodation targeted at different sectors of the market. A serviced accommodation could be anything from a luxury home in a tranquil location, a luxury penthouse in a city centre, to a modest apartment or family home.

The advantage SA has over a buy-to-let or HMO is that it can work in locations where they don't. It is important to undertake some market research to find out why there is a specific demand for any given area, and make best use of the available systems and platforms to maximise the marketing and occupancy levels. SA is also more flexible in terms of the type of property that is suitable; it is generally more suited to properties with fewer bedrooms. As a rule of thumb, SA works tends to work best with four or less bedrooms, where an HMO needs to have four or more.

How Does The Serviced Accommodation Strategy Work?

Set up your business structure in consultation with your specialist property accountant and tax advisor. This is particularly important with serviced accommodation as there are capital allowances available, which can make a huge difference to tax.

- **Select your prime location and goldmine area** in which to operate your SA properties. It is important that you understand the area.
- **Find a suitable property** – An SA can be operated from: property

that you own, you are looking to purchase, or property that you do not own but you are looking to control under a rent-to-rent agreement. SAs generally work best on properties with one to four bedrooms. The property is let on a nightly, weekly or up to one-month basis, which results in a higher rental income from the property. It is important to note that there are also higher expenses involved in operating an SA.

- **Make an offer for the property (to buy or control it) if you do not already own it** – If you own, are looking to buy, or looking to control a property which you intend to operate an SA business from, it is important that the property is suitable; that it can be operated as an SA and that you have good legal contracts and agreements in place.

- **Set up the property** – There are also a number of rules and regulations which are on the increase that affect SA properties. It is important that you keep up to date with these changes in order to be compliant. Carry out any works required to the property in order to comply with rules and regulations, furnish the property and set up the utilities and broadband. It is important that you set up the property to be attractive to the type of tenants that you wish to attract.

- **Set up the systems** – With SA, the main systems to set up are marketing, pricing, booking management, payments, cleaning, laundry, maintenance, health & safety, etc.

- **Protect your property and business** – Have in place Property Ombudsman Registration, Data Protection Registration & Policy, and all relevant insurances,

- **Find guests** – Marketing the property well and achieving high occupancy levels is the key to the success of a SA. When marketing the property, it is important to understand what type of guest you wish to provide accommodation for. There are many platforms that you can use to market the property, the main ones being Booking.com and AirBnB, and also Expedia, Laterooms and many more.

There are four different levels and types of guests. It basically works the same as hotel ratings:

- **5 Star High-End** – Aimed at executives and tourists. This model provides 5 Star hotel suite type accommodation for high-end professionals or tourists in or near affluent parts of towns or cities, and therefore attracts the best tenants and commands the highest nightly rates. In order to attract high-end guests, the property needs to be furnished accordingly, which requires the largest initial investment. Provided it is set up and run well, it can be the most profitable cashflow model.
- **4 Star** – Aimed at professionals and tourists. This has less start-up and operating costs than the luxury end of the market. It is particularly suited to professionals and consultants during the week and leisure guests during the weekends.
- **3 Star** – Aimed at tourists and contractors. This can be a lucrative sector when large projects are being undertaken, and may not necessarily need to be right in the town centre where prices are often higher. These can be located close to the main industry of the town/city, for example near a hospital, large manufacturing plant or large construction project. Guests are less fussy about the quality of the accommodation.
- **2 Star Tourist** – This is suited to tourists and contractors looking for short term simple, clean and comfortable accommodation on a budget.

Repeat and scale what works until you reach your financial and lifestyle goals.

In order to analyse a serviced accommodation deal, it is important to consider the fixed costs; which need to be paid regardless of whether the property is occupied or not, and the variable costs; which are related to the costs of a guest or guests occupying the property, such as cleaning and laundry costs. The anticipated profit or loss can then be calculated on varying occupancy levels. Occupancy levels can be difficult to determine accurately and therefore profit levels are the same. A typical serviced accommodation property will break even around 30 to 40% occupancy and should be able to achieve a 70%+ occupancy level. Having a good strategy to maximise the occupancy levels through the winter months can make a huge difference to the profit levels and overall success of a serviced accommodation business.

It is important to understand that VAT is applicable on serviced accommodation, so when your turnover hits the VAT turnover level, where you will be required to become VAT registered, this will affect your deal analysis. The current VAT Registration threshold is £85,000.

Serviced accommodation is a high-cashflow property trading strategy, which when set up and managed well, can be a very lucrative business. Like all strategies, it has its advantages and disadvantages.

Advantages:

- It is suitable for the rent-to-rent model, where you don't need to own or buy property.
- High cashflow.
- Cashflow is positive as payments are made upfront.
- Can work in locations where other strategies don't.
- Can work in properties which are not suitable for other strategies.
- Good strategy for those who enjoy providing a guest experience.
- No tenants.
- No bad debt, provided you take payment upfront or on arrival.
- Can be suitable and good for JV deals with property owner or outside partners.

Disadvantages:

- Demand can be low in the winter months.
- Time intensive.
- Management intensive.
- Marketing intensive.

- Operationally intensive.
- High maintenance.
- Little time to repair any damage to property between guests arriving.
- Lots of paperwork.
- Dealing with guest complaints.

PROPERTY STRATEGY 5
SOURCING AND PACKAGING DEALS

Search for good property deals.	Keep deal for self. Package deal to others.	Buy. Hold. Package. Transfer.

Sourcing Property Deals

Having the ability to spot a good investment opportunity in your prime location and goldmine area can make you a fortune and comes from a combination of factors:

- **Knowledge** – Be prepared and armed with knowledge to be in pole position to spot and take advantage of opportunities.
- **Experience** – The more experience you have the better, but where you lack experience, leverage the knowledge and experience of your power team.
- **Action** – How active you are at promoting yourself as the go-to property expert in your prime location and goldmine area.
- **Connections** – How well connected you are. Remember to build your network before you need it. Your network = Your net worth.

The more you focus on an area and the more active you become with it, the greater the level of expertise you will gain, which in turn increases the chances of you finding and attracting great opportunities. Focusing on your personal and business branding is an important part of becoming the go-to expert in your area.

The golden opportunities with any strategy are generally found in off-market opportunities. Success in finding these opportunities comes down to a blend of hunger, knowledge, experience, patience and the quality and breadth of your power team.

The amateur investors are typically full of hunger and desperation, and therefore tend to pay too much for deals. The more established property investors tend to lose some of their hunger over time, but develop greater patience and knowledge of the numbers. Having the right balance of hunger and patience is important.

> *"Opportunities Are Everywhere – Around 20% Of Property Transactions In The UK Are Off-Market Opportunities."*
> **– Calum Kirkness**

There are two main reasons for sourcing deals:

1. **Sourcing deals for yourself** – this is the best route to finding the best deals. Any deals that you find and don't want for yourself, you can package and sell to other investors for a fee.
2. **Sourcing deals for other investors** - You can focus purely on sourcing deals to package and pass on to other investors or operators for a fee. This is a good strategy for beginners with only a small amount of start-up capital available. They can then use the proceeds to work their way up to more advanced strategies that require more initial upfront investment.

There are five main types of deals that you can look to source for investors:

1. Below Market Value Properties
2. Purchase Lease Options
3. Rent-To-Rent HMO
4. Rent-To-Rent SA
5. Development Opportunities – For example, land or commercial to residential conversions.

It is important to establish your sourcing criteria.

One of the secrets to becoming a deal-sourcing expert is to find your niche and get laser focused on it. Become the go-to expert in your prime location and goldmine area and promote yourself as much as you can.

Once you have established which strategy and investor type you are going to focus on, you can then focus on finding the best properties that match your own or investors' cashflow and/or capital appreciation goals.

> *"Business Is Simple, Do Not Over Complicate It By Adopting A Scattergun Approach. Go An Inch Wide And Mile Deep Rather Than A Mile Wide And An Inch Deep."*
> **– Calum Kirkness**

There Are Two Ways To Source Deals:

1. Direct to vendor; which is the ideal and best way.
2. Via a third party.

The Top Three Strategies To Source Direct To Vendor Are:

1. Leafleting.
2. Direct letter.
3. Bandit board – Be careful with this option as you could be in breach of local authority rules and be asked to remove the boards, possibly facing a fine.

Let's Look At Direct Leafletting First:

1. Design and print 5,000 A5 size simple leaflets using the AIDA marketing design principle. AIDA is short for Attention – Interest – Desire – Action. First you want to grab the person's attention, then you want to keep their interest, then build desire focusing on what's in it for them, and finally have a clear call to action of what step you want them to take next.
2. Deliver the leaflets yourself or hire a person or company to do

deliver them for you. The leaflets should be strategically distributed in your goldmine area, ideally missing out any properties that you know are owned by the local authority or a housing association.

3. Place the same leaflet in as many shops, businesses and public spaces in your goldmine area as possible; always get the property owner's permission.

4. Deliver the same leaflets to the same properties every two weeks on an ongoing basis.

5. Always have your leaflets delivered separately to any other mail.

6. Track and measure the distribution and all responses to establish what is working.

Direct Letter Strategy:

This strategy takes more time and effort than leafletting, due to the information required, but it is a more targeted strategy that can be effective.

1. Go to your local or online stationery outlet and purchase:
   a. Yellow A4 paper.
   b. Red pens.
   c. Black pens.
   d. Plain white, yellow or eye-catching envelopes, i.e. white with a red band around the outside.
   e. 1st or 2nd class stamps, ideally 2nd class.

2. Hand-write a letter in red pen, on yellow paper using the AIDA principal. Then, place it in the envelope with the address written in black pen, and put a stamp on the envelope.

The object is to create curiosity, which will lead to prospects looking at the leaflet or opening up the letter and reading it.

Before distributing the leaflets and sending out the letters, be ready for the calls. Know your pitch and script on what information you require and how you can help your prospect.

Get Ready And Expect To Receive Three Types Of Call From:

1. **Mr Angry** – Go away and stop putting leaflets in my door or writing letters to me.
2. **Mr Curious** – Thanks for the letter, but I'm not sure if it's for me.
3. **Mr Happy** – I would like to know more about how you can help me.

A great way to increase your conversion rate is to educate and train yourself in basic sales techniques.

Top 12 Places To Source Deals Via Third Party:

1. Always be personally on the look-out when travelling around.
2. Online property portals like Rightmove, Zoopla, etc.
3. Via Estate Agents.
4. Via Letting Agents.
5. Auction Houses.
6. Government and local authority websites.
7. NHS Properties.
8. Newspaper.
9. Networking.
10. Facebook.
11. LinkedIn.
12. HMO Licencing register from Local Authority.

Property sourcing for investors or operators can be a great beginner's strategy and a great way to get started if you have limited knowledge, experience and funds. It is easy to learn, requires low investment, can easily be implemented around other commitments and produce a nice income; which can replace your current income relatively quickly depending on your level of commitment.

In recent years there has been a trend of people calling themselves 'property sourcers' and 'deal packagers'. This is due to the increase in the number of property training events. The market is full of them, but don't let this put you off. Most of the property sourcers do not have the knowledge or experience to understand what a good deal is or how to package it correctly and attractively to an investor.

The Basic Process Of Property Sourcing Is As Follows:

- You send out marketing material; normally an A5 size leaflet or direct letter, to find motivated people who need to sell their house fast due to their current circumstances.
- The owner/seller of the property contacts you via telephone and you pre-qualify them over the phone before arranging to meet them in person at the property.
- If it is a below market value deal, you agree a purchase price with them for the property, which is ideally at least 25% less than the current market value.
- If it is a rent-to-rent deal, either for HMO or SA, agree a fixed monthly fee, rental period and conditions, which are attractive to the property owner and will also be attractive to anyone looking to control but not own a property and operate an HMO or SA business.
- Once the deal has been prepared, prepare a lockout agreement which gives you sole exclusivity to the deal for a period of two to three months in order to find an investor who is looking for such deals.
- You find an investor or operator, or ideally have ones already lined up looking to buy property or operate an HMO or SA in that area.
- You give the investor or operator the deal and they complete on the sale or deal and take ownership or control of the property.
- The investor or operator pays you a finder's fee for the deal which, in the case of a BMV deal, will vary on quality of the deal but can typically be between £3,000 to £5,000. With the rent-to-rent deals, the fee might typically range from £1,000 to £5,000.
- Keep repeating, refining and improving the process and scale what works.
- Keep it simple.

With property sourcing and deal packaging, you can replace your current income and be earning over £5,000 to £10,000 per month with very little effort by systemising the process. This can then allow you to outsource some parts of the process to a Virtual Assistant (VA) if you choose. You may have heard the term 'VA' before, and it generally involves hiring people in a different country such as the Philippines, which is a particularly popular destination for people in the UK to source to a VA. You can learn more about outsourcing services if you attend our property training days and events.

The best strategy to start out with is finding and packaging BMV Deals as they are the easiest for investors and vendors to understand. Once you have mastered BMV Sourcing and increased your knowledge, experience and investment funds you can progress to the other types of sourcing and property strategies.

Packaging The Deals To Investors:

In order to make an income and get paid for sourcing deals it is important to understand how to package and sell the deal on to an investor. The basic process is as follows:

1. Present your deal in a professional, clear and standardized format to your investor/buyer with details of your sourcing fee (e.g. £5,000).
2. The potential buyer confirms that they would like to secure the deal.
3. Take a deposit (e.g. £1,000) from the investor in order for you to take the deal off the market.
4. Allow the solicitors to do the legal process, which is the same as any normal house sale.
5. Upon exchange of contracts between the vendor's and the buyer's solicitors, the buyer pays you the remaining sourcing fee (eg. £4,000).

Packaging A Deal To A Retail Buyer

If you can source and package a deal to a retail investor, which is someone looking to purchase a home for themselves rather than as an investment property, they will generally be happy with a lower discount meaning you can increase your profit from each deal.

PROPERTY STRATEGY 6
PURCHASE LEASE OPTIONS

Search for good property deals.	Lease / control property. Rent property out or package deal and sell to others.	Control. Rent. Buy. Transfer.

What Is A Purchase Lease Option

A purchase lease option is a legal contract between the property owner and the property investor, which allows the property investor to control the property with an option, but not the obligation, to purchase the property for an agreed and fixed price at an agreed and specified date in the future or at any point within the option period. What this means is the investor can control the property and rent it out to generate a positive cashflow income without the need to have a large deposit and purchase the property from the start, but have the option to purchase the property at a later agreed date or walk away from the deal when the agreement expires. The advantage to the property owner is that the option allows them to move on with their life when they are in negative equity and cannot afford to sell the property.

Most people who are selling a property are doing so to raise money for some reason. Property owners with a mortgage value which is higher than the value of the property find themselves in negative equity, so selling to release funds is not an option. They are unable to sell unless they can make up the difference to pay off the mortgage liability and meet the selling costs from savings.

Property owners who find themselves in this situation often feel stuck with a large burden on their shoulders. When a property investor comes along with the solution of purchase lease option allowing the property owner to move on without financial penalty, this can come as a welcome relief to them.

We can see that purchase lease options can provide a win-win solution for both the current owner and the investor.

The purchase lease option strategy tends to work best when the market is upside down and property values are falling. The rental market tends to grow during recessions.

The challenge with purchase lease options is that they can be difficult to explain, and many people are sceptical of them, believing them to sound too good to be true!

The best way to explain them is to give an example:

Current Property Owner's Situation – The Problem

Mr Smith bought a house one year ago for £100,000 with a 95% mortgage = £95,000.

The value of Mr Smith's property has dropped by 10% due to market conditions to £90,000.

Mr Smith is now in what is termed negative equity, where the value of the property is less than the mortgage secured on it. He has a mortgage of £95,000 and a property valued at £90,000, which means he has negative equity of £5,000.

Mr Smith's circumstances have changed, and he would like to sell the property but is unable to do so because he has no savings.

For him to sell, he would need to have £5,000 to pay off the balance of the mortgage, plus meet the selling costs to release himself from his responsibility, obligations and liabilities.

Mr Smith has secured a new job and needs to move areas.

Mr Smith sees a leaflet from Mr Joe Bloggs, property investor, and contacts him.

How You Can Help Mr Smith As A Property Investor:

As a smart property investor, Mr Bloggs understands Mr Smith's position, the property market, property values, rental prices and rental demand.

Mr Bloggs has carried out his due diligence and assessed that there is good rental demand in the area, the figures stack up and the area has good potential for capital growth as the market recovers.

The Solution To The Problem

Mr Bloggs, property investor, meets with Mr Smith and proposes a purchase lease option.

Mr Bloggs proposes a deal to offer Mr Smith £1 to take control of the property with the option, but not the obligation, to purchase the property for £100,000 in 5 years' time. In order to make the purchase lease option legal there needs to be a legal consideration, which is usually £1, but can be more depending on the individual circumstances for the owner and investor.

Mr Bloggs also advises Mr Smith that he will pay a guaranteed monthly amount, which more than covers Mr Smith's mortgage payments, leaving him with a small surplus each month.

This option is attractive to Mr Smith as it relieves him of the burden of his current situation of being unable to afford to sell the property and move on with his life.

You might ask if Mr Bloggs can make a positive cashflow from the property, why would Mr Smith not rent the property out himself and benefit from positive cashflow? It's a very good question and there are several reasons why a property owner wouldn't want to do this:

- They do not want the hassle or risk of being a landlord.
- They are worried about bad tenants.
- They are worried about void periods.
- There may be a negative association with the property for them and they want to move on with their life.
- The property owner's loss is unlimited.

The Main Advantage To The Property Owner For Granting An Investor A Property Lease Option Is:

- They receive guaranteed rental income payment from the investor each month, regardless of whether the property has a tenant or not. For some people this peace of mind and security is more important.
- They can achieve a positive monthly cashflow, which can be especially attractive if they have a mortgage with relatively low interest.
- They do not need to come up with the money to pay off the shortfall in the mortgage if they sold the property.
- They do not need to come up with the money to pay the selling fees if they were to sell the property.
- They get the full value of the property some time in the future.
- They may still benefit from a share of the rise in value of the property depending on the terms of the agreement.
- They may get an upfront payment depending on the terms of the agreement.

The Advantages For Mr Bloggs, Property Investor, Are As Follows:

- Allows him to bypass the often deal-breaking surveyors and mortgage lenders.
- There is no need for a large deposit.
- It creates opportunity to generate cashflow with very little investment.

- It provides an opportunity to benefit from capital appreciation if the property value increases, without the risk of owning the property.
- The investor's losses are limited.
- An option to purchase instead of buying allows you flexibility, much lower costs than a buy and sell, and avoids having to wait six months to re-mortgage.

There are many variables when it comes to structuring a property lease option, which can include an initial lump sum payment from the investor at the start and a share of any capital appreciation if the value of the property rises. The duration of the lease can also vary a lot. Some investors like to keep the period of the purchase lease option short: three to five years, whilst other investors prefer longer agreement periods: five to ten years, or up to a maximum of the remaining term of the mortgage.

Property lease options are a tried and tested financial strategy that is being applied and put into action every day, all over the world.

How To Spot And Find A Potential Purchase Lease Option Deal

- When a vendor has their property advertised both with an estate agent for sale and a letting agent for rent at the same time, it could indicate that they would ideally like to sell but may be struggling to find a buyer, and therefore willing to rent their property until they can sell. With a purchase lease option, you are proposing to offer them a solution to do exactly that by paying them a guaranteed monthly rent until you buy the property at some time in the future.
- Another type of vendor is the tired landlord, who is tired of the hassle of renting out their properties. As they are already investors with knowledge of the property sector, they are more likely to be open to creative solutions.

The ideal scenario is finding the deals direct to vendor using some of the sourcing strategies, which we have already covered, or they can also be found via estate agents and lettings agents.

The Legal Agreements And Contracts For A Purchase Lease Option

Once you have discussed and set out the basis for any purchase lease option, it is important that both the investor and the vendor have their own legal representation, to ensure that all parties fully understand the terms of the agreement that they are entering into, and there needs to be a financial consideration to make the contract legal, which can be as low as £1.

For the investor, one of the main benefits of a purchase lease option is that they have the right but not the obligation to buy the property at an agreed time in the future. For example, in 5 years' time: imagine the value of the property has gone up by £40,000 during that time, and the vendor has changed their mind and no longer wants to sell the property to the investor claiming that they didn't understand the agreement or felt forced in to it. Therefore, it is important for both parties to have independent legal advice when the contracts are being produced and signed.

As property lease option agreements are relatively new in the residential sector, a lot of solicitors do not understand them and are therefore unable to assist or put their clients off entering into one. This is where having a good power team comes into play, where you have specialists in place to arrange the contracts. It is advisable to have at least two sets of different legal practices in place, who have specialists in purchase lease options, where one can act for the investor and you can recommend the other to the vendor. All you need to do as the investor is agree the heads of terms with the vendor and pass them on to the solicitors to draw up the legal contracts.

The Heads Of Terms Should Include:

- The investor's full name and address.
- The vendor's full name and address.
- The address of the property that the agreement relates to.
- The agreed option fee, which needs to be a minimum of £1.
- The option agreement period.

- The monthly lease payment.
- Any other special terms and conditions.

Depending on the terms and conditions of the purchase lease option agreement and several other factors relating to the property title, the mortgage and the area, lease options can offer options in terms of what the investor can do with the property during the lease option period.

For example:

- The investor may decide to live there themselves.
- Add value to the property and flip it for profit.
- Use the property for HMO or SA, which is very similar to the rent-to-rent strategy.
- Control an overseas property. This can be beneficial to vendors who have purchased an overseas property and no longer want to live there but are unable to sell it.

Property purchase lease options can be a great strategy that provides both vendors and investors with win-win solutions in various circumstances.

PROPERTY STRATEGY 7
PROPERTY DEVELOPMENT – BUILD-TO-SELL AND BUILD-TO-RENT

Search for good property development opportunities – land or existing commercial & larger residential property.	Build new properties / buy large existing residential properties and split them into smaller separate units. Convert existing non-residential properties to residential properties.	Sell & take profit. Hold & rent for Cashflow And Capital Growth

How Does Property Development Work?

Property developers typically buy and sell and realise a profit on completion of the development. However, some prefer to build and hold the properties and add them to their property portfolio, in which case they should have equity of 20%+ in the property.

Property developers make a profit by bringing together all the individual parts to complete the development at a cost less than the market value of the completed development.

Four Strategies That Developers Use To Develop Properties Are:

- Buying greenfield land, which is zoned for development, and build new properties on it.

- Buying existing commercial buildings and converting them into multiple residential buildings.
- Buying brownfield development sites, demolish the existing buildings and develop new properties on the site.
- Buying existing residential properties, typically large properties in a rundown state, and transform them into single or multiple new units.

Many people that I speak to about property investment and trading, have the goal of ultimately becoming a property developer. It is one of the more complex property strategies, which even the experienced professionals get wrong sometimes, but when designed and managed well and carried out at the right time in the right market conditions, can be a very rewarding strategy.

Experienced property developers have an inner circle of trusted contacts who may bring them deals and are only a phone call away when there is a problem that needs solving.

But what if you're starting from scratch? The solution is two-fold:

1. Firstly, you commit to improving your knowledge through **education**.

2. Secondly, creating detailed **checklists and systems** to manage the many variables in developing property. We will look at this in more detail later in the chapter.

Optional: Invest in a property coach or mentor to guide you through the process, and access their systems and checklists. These can be very valuable documents to have and save a lot of time, headaches and costly errors.

If you have always wanted to become a property developer but felt that you lacked the knowledge, experience and contacts to get started, property development could be for you if you:

- Have access to funds/equity that you would like to reinvest.
- Have land/property which you own outright, or have little borrowing against but little or no cash to develop it.

- Own land with development potential.
- Have a house situated on a large plot of land where there is room to potentially build an additional property or properties.
- Want to grow your property portfolio quicker.

If any of these sound like you, property development could be a good strategy for you to develop properties at cost price.

When you develop property, you get to keep the profit or add the new property to your portfolio at cost price and have some equity in the development.

Property Development Is Complex With Many Pitfalls. In Order To Be Successful And Make A Profit, It Is Very Important To Understand The Numbers And The Process.

Before We Go In To More Details Of The Property Development Process, Let's Have A Quick Look At Some Of The Numbers From A Development – For Illustration And Guidance Purposes Only.

Property Development Deal Calculator	Amount	Amount
Forecast gross development value	**£1,200,000**	
Forecast gross development costs	**£900,000**	
Land cost (approximately (15 to 50%)		
TDC: Total development costs. Say 25%. Land cost for this example =		£225,000
Buying costs (0.5-3% TDC). Say 1%		£9,000
Consultants (3-5% of TDC). Say 3%		£27,000
Investigations (1-3% TDC). Say 1%		£9,000
Construction cost (59% of TDC).		£531,000
Finance Costs (6-18% TDC). Say 8%		£72,000
Selling costs (2%-5%of TDC). Say 3%		£27,000
Total development costs		**£900,000**
Developer's margin (15-35% of GDV)		
Say 25% developer's margin	**£300,000**	

Once the development in the example above is complete, the developer can choose to sell and pocket £300,000 as profit, which they may want to use to finance the next project, or they can hold the property and have £300,000 of equity in the development. This is like buying brand new properties at a 25% BMV discount (market value of property £1,200,000 and total development costs £900,000) which is equal to a 25% discount or profit.

What I have found over my years in business, property investment and property development is that systems are more reliable than depending on close associates. Systems bring a level of science to the process that even many experienced developers don't have. I teach these systems and checklist in my full Property Success Development training.

> *"Systems Run Your Business, People Run Your Systems."*
> **– Calum Kirkness**

Until you create systems, you will never free up your own time.

It is your job as the developer to stack the odds in your favour to ensure they go well.

How The Property Development Process Works:

Property development is where you take the various individual parts – land, building planning, engineering, materials, designs, labour, finance, marketing, selling and so on – and create a product worth more than the sum of its parts. When you master the process, you master the ability to manufacture profits through property development.

Step 1 – Decide and Commit

The first, and the most difficult, step to take when starting out is making the decision to take action and just do it. Being clear about what you want and believing 100% that you can achieve it is important.

Step 2 – Market Analysis

It is essential to carry out market analysis to ensure you are developing a property that has demand, is built to the standard that would appeal to the new buyer and fetch the price you expect. There is no point developing a new building when your market analysis tells you there are lots of other projects coming up in the same street or area.

Your Market Analysis Should Include Factors Such As:

- What's already being built in the neighbourhood?
- Who are the developers building it?
- What are their prices? (You get a lot of this information by simply picking up the phone and talking with people.)
- Working drawings, specification and ideally quantities, will allow you to get reasonably accurate budget quotes from builders. This is also a good opportunity for you to build relationships with potential suppliers and contractors. Be nice to them: suppliers and builders tend to get a lot of tyre kickers who waste their time. Giving a builder precise information will show that you are serious and encourage them to help you. Make sure to contact several builders and get at least three budget costs. You are likely to come across some "interesting" characters to deal with. But it's important not to pre-judge anyone. Not all builders are out to get you and having several good builders in your power team can become one of your best assets as a property developer.
- What is the design intent in the local area? Before you begin a development it is important to know what buyers are looking for. For example, do they want three bedrooms, two bathrooms + study, or would they pay more for a bespoke unique living design because the plot has beautiful sea views. The best person to answer this question is a local estate agent who has sold similar properties. A few phone calls or drop-in meetings at the local estate agencies will give you a wealth of valuable information.
- What is the demand for this type of design in your area?

- What would be the end value of your planned property type? Once again, local estate agents can give you this information. And you can find valuable, up-to-date information online.
- What is the rental demand and yields in the current market for your planned property type?
- What are comparable sales in the nearby area? Having this information will allow you to make wise design and investment decisions. Without this information you will be guessing, which is not a good idea.

Step 3 – Feasibility Analysis

Feasibility analysis is like a business plan, it is an important factor in determining the viability of a project and whether it receives your initial tick of approval or if any of the parts need further negotiation or get rejected. A feasibility analysis reveals all the costs involved in completing the project. While it will include some assumptions, everything must be based on sound research and facts. Avoid the temptation to introduce subjective emotion to your financial planning, which could result in an expensive mistake and lesson.

Many successful developers will tell you that it's the projects they didn't do that made the difference to their success.

The feasibility analysis will also form the basis of a loan application. Lenders will know if there are any gaps or holes in the feasibility analysis and financial planning and ask for an explanation of any assumptions and reasons behind the numbers. If they suspect that the feasibility has not been done well, they will not only decline the loan but you will also lose credibility and potentially damage a relationship with an important funding partner. Good banking contacts are a valuable resource to have.

Checking assumptions with facts and data is a big part of my approach, which is why I created my Property Success Insider Development Feasability Calculator, which gives a basic feasibility analysis and a yes or no answer in minutes, to determine if the opportunity is worthy of further investigation or not.

Step 4 – Due Diligence

Due diligence is a comprehensive process that must be carried out correctly to satisfy legal requirements and ascertain the risks and advantages of a specific development. It will include legal searches and title checks conducted by a conveyancer or solicitor, inquiries into the external requirements that may be involved (e.g. town planning issues like zoning, density, setbacks, heights, neighbourhood character, landscaping, etc.) and an analysis to determine the best use of the land, which may involve an architect and town planner. Having a good relationship with a town planner and architect, and having them as part of your power team can be a valuable resource.

Some of the site-specific issues to consider include:

- **Total site area:** This must be checked carefully as a few extra square metres could mean the difference between the number of properties and having enough parking spaces, and the difference between profit and loss.
- **Usable area:** It is vital to understand the total area that can be used for building, and the set-back requirements, as these factors can limit the extend and viability of the development. Density is measured as a percentage of the total site area and will typically vary depending on location.
- **Topography:** The slope of the site is another important factor to consider if the site is suitable for development or not. An ideal site is flat or has a slight fall to allow for storm water run-off. Developing a sloping site is generally more expensive, particularly where retaining walls are required, and accessing sloping sites can put some buyers off. Sites that slope towards the street are often considered better than those that fall away as vehicle access is easier.

Step 5 – Design, Planning Permission and Building Regulations and Permits

- When buying a property, the three most important factors to keep in mind are: LOCATION, LOCATION, LOCATION.
- Similarly, when you are about to develop property, you should think of another three: COUNCIL, COUNCIL, COUNCIL. Councils can be your greatest ally, or they can be difficult to deal with when trying to gain permission for your development.
- The key is to balance the best possible use for the land with the council guidelines. Delays to the planning process can be time-consuming and costly. There is the option to appeal the council decision, but I would advise against this if possible due to the time it takes. Councils are there for a reason, and it is always best to work within the boundaries of the town plan.

Local Authority Permissions, Warrants and Permits are a statement of consent that allows a particular use of the land. There are three main items you are required to have in place prior to starting:

I. **Planning Permission** deals with town planning and whether the proposed use and design of the development for a piece of land is appropriate. For further details on planning, see the chapter on permissions and protection.

II. **Building Regulations Approval** follows planning permission and deals with the design of the actual building. For further details on building regulations, see the chapter on permissions and protection.

III. **Structural Engineering Design and Certification** – This is linked with the Building Regulations Approval and deals with engineering design such as drainage, earthworks, road works, sewerage and water.

Once all the permits are in place, the construction work can begin.

Step 6 – Producing Contract Documents and Tendering the Project

Property development projects are either tendered via open tender; where the contract is advertised for contractors to express an interest and apply to be on the tender list, or via select tender; where the property developer selects or works with their preferred contractors.

Prior to tendering the construction, it is important to consider which form of construction contract you wish to use. There are various options available. Let's briefly look at each type of contract:

- **Traditional Form of Contract** – This is where there is a full set of construction drawings, a Bill of Quantities and a specification. With this type of contract, the developer retains all design responsibility and most of the risk.
- **Construction Management** – This is where owner builders hire construction managers to build the development or their single dwelling. This is common for very large construction sites, or when an owner builder is building their own house.
- **Cost Plus Contract** – This type of contract usually has no upper limit, which in turn does not motivate the contractor to be economical.
- **Design & Build (D&B)** – This is where the contractor does everything from hiring consultants to designing the project. The owner can still accept or reject the design but is no longer responsible for coordinating or managing. Once the design is approved, the contractor supervises and carries out the construction.
- **Lump-Sum, Fixed Price or Turn-key Contracts** – These are the most common for small to medium-size developers. As the term suggests, they are fixed price in the sense that they have a set price for a specified scope. Lenders like this type of contract because there are no hidden surprises and fewer risks. If the scope of the project changes in any way, these changes can be added to the price in the form of a variation. It is best to avoid variations

during the construction phase as they can lead to uneconomical cost and time increases.

- **Self Build** - Buying your own materials, hiring plant and selecting your own sub-contractors can be the most cost-effective method of property development but requires the developer to have an indepth knowledge of the complete development and construction process as well as having excellent project management skills.

An important part of any project is having as much detailed information available to tender the works and award the construction contract(s). The more accurate and detailed the documents, the easier the procurement process will be and the more accurate the tender returns from the contractors will be. The important documents to include in tender and contract award packages are:

- Site investigation survey and investigation reports.
- Detailed construction drawings.
- Design statement.
- Detailed mechanical and electrical services drawings.
- Specification.
- Any schedules.
- Bill of Quantities.
- Contract conditions.
- Construction programme (timeline of when the works will be started, carried out and completed).
- Risk register.
- Minutes of meetings.
- Any other business.

Any changes to the design after the works have commenced can be costly and give the contractor the opportunity to claim for cost variations which can also have time implications.

Step 7 – Development Finance

It is best to start enquiring about and sourcing finance for a development after the full-scale feasibility analysis has been completed. Once you have determined the equity and cash you can access, and potentially who else can contribute funds, it is time to start sourcing finance. There are several development finance options available. Funding your deals is covered in Chapter 11.

Step 8 – Off-Plan Marketing

You can start marketing and selling the development as soon as permits have been granted. The larger the project, the more important pre-selling off-plan in the early stages of construction becomes. Every pre-sale you achieve offsets your level of debt, which in turn reduces the risk in the project. Waiting to sell the finished stock just before or after completion can be a good option when economic times are good and the market is rising.

Sometimes the cost of holding the property is outweighed by the capital gains the market can present. The risk and rewards need to be balanced and an informed decision made.

Step 9 – Construction Phase

Once all permission and permits have been obtained the construction works can legally commence, and the contractor can be appointed and given the go ahead to start the works.

As soon as all the permission and permits are in place to allow the works to commence, it is important to get the contractor to start the works as soon as possible. Time = Money.

During the construction phase, it is important to monitor and manage the contractor and works to ensure that the works are being carried out in accordance with the contract documents. This includes following the correct design and specification, building to the desired quality standards, carrying out the works in a safe manner, which complies with Health and Safety regulations and carrying out the works on time and in accordance with the construction programme.

It is advisable to hold regular scheduled meetings with the contractor during the construction phase to deal with any issues in a timely manner. If you have the relevant knowledge and experience, you can choose to manage the project yourself or appoint a project manager and quantity surveyor to manage progress and costs on your behalf. It is a good idea to shadow what they are doing so that you can do this yourself on future projects if that is something that you would like to do; if it isn't, you have at least increased your knowledge and experience.

Valuations also need to be made to determine the value of the works that have been carried out to date, which is normally monthly, and ensure the contractor is paid in a timely manner for the works carried out in accordance with the contract documents.

STEP 10 – Obtaining Final Completion Certification and Registrations

In order to complete the project and settle the sales it is essential to have all the completion certificates, registrations and titles in place:

- Building Regulations Compliance Completion Certificate.
- Certificate of Occupancy.
- Any building warranties that are being provided.
- Issue of titles.
- Any other business.

The final stage is completion of the sale of all the units and collecting the profit from your efforts. The aim of property development is to be in a better financial position than when you started.

Property development is like the buy-to-flip strategy; the tips shared in that section apply to property development, and the information in this section is valuable to the buy-to-flip process.

PROPERTY SUCCESS INSIDER

7 STEP PROPERTY DEVELOPMENT FORMULA - DESIGNED TO LIFT YOUR PROFITS

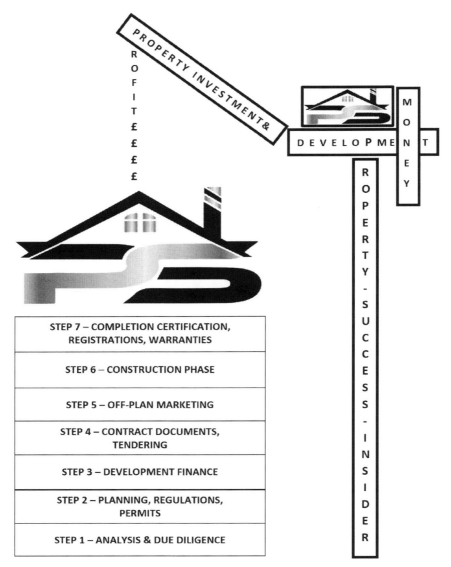

STEP 7 – COMPLETION CERTIFICATION, REGISTRATIONS, WARRANTIES

STEP 6 – CONSTRUCTION PHASE

STEP 5 – OFF-PLAN MARKETING

STEP 4 – CONTRACT DOCUMENTS, TENDERING

STEP 3 – DEVELOPMENT FINANCE

STEP 2 – PLANNING, REGULATIONS, PERMITS

STEP 1 – ANALYSIS & DUE DILIGENCE

PROPERTY STRATEGY 8
HANDS-OFF INVESTOR

Search for good property investment opportunities.

Provide investment funding to investor on agreed terms.

Investment funds repaid back to you in accordance with funding agreement.

What Is A Hands-Off Investor?

If you have funds to invest and are looking to put your money to work with a hands-off property investment, then providing funding to property investors can provide attractive returns.

There is always an abundance of property investors and traders looking for short to medium-term finance to fund deals. They are often required to act fast in order to secure these deals and therefore unable to, or don't have the time, to follow the more conventional finance options.

As a guide, the typical current average rate of return being offered by those in the property sector on short-term property investments ranges from 6% to 18%+ per annum pro-rata, or they may include a percentage of the profit from the deal, an equity stake or a combination of all. Being in the position to provide immediate cash funding puts you in a strong position to negotiate terms. The terms can, and should, be assessed and negotiated based on the level of risk involved and the security that can be offered. The less security offered, the riskier the investment.

One good rule of investing is to only invest in what you understand and believe in. Even if you do not intend to invest directly in property yourself, or trade in any of the strategies, it is a good idea to keep yourself educated on all the latest strategies and news in the sector in order to be able to negotiate good and fair deals, which maximise your return whilst minimising your risk.

- Always do your own due diligence on the individual and company looking for the loan and the details of the deal.
- It should be noted that property investment is not covered by FCA and does not offer the same level of protection as some other investment types.
- It is also important to ensure that all investments are covered by legally binding signed contracts to ensure that all the parties understand what they are getting into.

Providing you understand how the property sector works and understand and carry out thorough due diligence, being a hands-off investor can provide a nice, easy return on your money without all the other hassles that are typically associated with property.

There are many other strategies such as delayed completion and assisted sale, which are forms and combinations of the strategies shared. There really is no end to how creative you can be. Where there is a problem, there is always a solution.

CHAPTER 4

SELECTING YOUR PROPERTY STRATEGY

The joint most important step when starting out on your property journey is to identify and select your preferred property strategy that is the right fit for YOU. It must be closely considered and selected along with the right location, which is covered in the next chapter. Not all strategies work in all locations.

A lot of people come to me today asking which property strategy they should choose. They are being informed and influenced by others to follow a certain strategy, or they are following the media headlines and reading that some property strategies are dead, whilst other strategies are being termed as the new alternative strategy to follow.

The truth is that there are many property strategies which work today. The key is choosing the one that is right for you, the one that best fits your character and can help you reach your goals, and not necessarily the strategy that is being suggested by others. This chapter covers several key fundamentals to consider in helping you choose the best strategy for you.

Let me give you an example to illustrate my point.

Let's say Person A is the world #1 snooker player, they are winning a lot of competitions and prize money and earning a nice income from exhibition events and sponsorship.

Person B is the world #1 darts player, who is also winning a lot of competitions and prize money and earning a nice income from exhibition events and sponsorship.

Person B meets up with Person A and tells them that they should switch their strategy and get into snooker, as there is more money in it than darts. Whilst this may be true, it is only true for those at the top of the game, and the darts player would end up earning less and maybe not even enjoy the game.

The best property strategy for you is the one which you enjoy and fits with your strengths.

Property Strategy Selection Formula – 9 Key Personal Factors To Consider:

1. Are You Investing For Cashflow, Capital Growth Or Both?

Some people in property will advise you to invest for cashflow rather than capital growth. I believe that the best strategy is a combination of ensuring that the monthly figures stack up for good positive cashflow and that the property is in a good location to achieve capital growth. I have seen people buy cheap high-yielding property which produces good cashflow, but the property hasn't increased in value at all and would probably take some time to sell. Other investors are prepared to sacrifice some cashflow for potential capital growth and will have still achieved good cashflow and great capital appreciation on a property that would be easy to sell.

I like to invest in properties that can produce a balanced combination of good cashflow and potential for capital appreciation.

Cashflow

- Cashflow is creating income now, whilst capital growth is creating future wealth.
- Cashflow can be made from property that you rent or control and property that you own.
- Cashflow is the difference between income and expenditure received each month. Income must exceed expenditure in order to survive, and ideally wherever possible income should be received before expenditure is made.
- There is investment wisdom in investing for cashflow. When a property has a positive cashflow, the investor is covered regardless of whether the value of the property goes up or down.

Capital Growth

There Are Three Ways To Benefit From Capital Growth In Property:

- Property value increases over time and you sell in the future for a profit. Statistically speaking, property will double in value every ten years. This has certainly not been the case over the last ten years from 2008 to 2018. In many areas, the prices are only just now getting back to the 2008 levels. However, if we look at property prices over a longer period of time, going back 100 years, we can see that property prices increase in value providing that you buy well. Your sole reason for owning a property should never be just about capital appreciation alone; if it is, you are a gambler!

- You buy the property which is below market value at the time of purchase and lock in some equity from day one, then you sell at a later date and release the profit. Let's say that you manage to buy a property 25% below market value, which means you have gained 25% capital growth from day one. If you had purchased a property valued at £100,000 in its current condition for £75,000, you have instantly gained £25,000 in equity. When you buy below market value, this achieves several things; if the property stays at the same value, you have made an instant capital gain; if property values drop, you have protected the downside and risk and increased your chances of getting your original investment back out if you need to sell during a downturn; if the property prices climb, you have a double gain. Buying well is the secret to success in property, which we will look at in more detail throughout the book.

- You add value to the property through renovation, refurbishment or extending it. Some people prefer to go for quick profit by buying up property which offers potential to add value, then carry out the works and sell the property on for a quick profit. It is known in the industry as fix and flip or buy-to-flip and has become a popular strategy, mainly due to property shows on television that show someone buying a property for a bargain price, fixing it up and selling it on for huge profits. It makes great TV, but it is not always as simple and straightforward as it looks!

2 – Identifying Your Personal Character

- Are you an introvert or extrovert?
- Are you a creative right brain thinker or logical left brain thinker?
- What is your attitude to risk – high, medium or low?
- Are you a dabbler, stressor or master?

The Dabbler Character – Has desire but no determination and no coach

The dabbler starts and improves but soon afterwards reaches a plateau. They continue for a little while but give up easily after seeing no further quick growth and believing that it is not for them; they try something else and repeat the same cycle. For a dabbler to break through and achieve new and improved results, it is important for them to have a coach or mentor at each stage who can help them up to the next level.

The Stressor Character – Has desire and determination but no coach

The stressor has the desire and the determination, but persists on their own without a coach. They push through the plateaus and get breakthroughs, but get burnt out. It takes them a long time to reach significantly high skill and result levels.

The Master Character – Has desire, has determination and has a coach

The master knows that they are going to hit challenges along the way and plateau at times but rather than struggle for the next breakthrough, they know that each time they hit one they need to find the right coach to continue to take them to the next level.

Do You Have Access To Funds – Your Own Or Others?

- Do you have your own funds – Yes or No?
- What level of your own funds do you have available – High, Medium or Low?

- Do you have access to other people's funds (Investors) – Yes or No?
- What level of investor funds do you have access to – High, Medium or Low?

If you do not have access to much of your own or investor funds, a great way to start is with a strategy that has a low investment entry level and produces cashflow like property sourcing or rent-to-rent, then start building up an investment fund which you can use to develop further strategies as you grow your knowledge, experience and funds.

3. How Much Time Do You Have Available?

What is your current time/employment position?

Are you:

- Working full-time with little available spare time?
- Working part-time and have some spare time available?
- Unemployed or retired and have lots free time available?

Are you happy with your current job and position and looking to do some property investment in your spare time, or are you looking to replace your current full-time employment through property and have more freedom in your life? This is a very important question to know the answer to.

Time is our most precious commodity and valuable asset.

"Rich Or Poor, We Are All Given The Same Amount Of Time Each Day. It Is How We Use The Time That We Are Given That Counts."
– Calum Kirkness

Imagine this... you have £86,400 cash in your hand right now and have no restrictions on how you can spend it.

Most people would be very happy to find themselves in this position and if they are wise, they would use it to invest in property.

*"We All Get 86,400 Seconds Of Time Each Day Deposited
In To Our Time Account –
It's Up To You How You Use Them."*
– Calum Kirkness

Time is our most valuable commodity and precious asset; we all wake up each morning with 86,400 seconds in our time account. Each morning, when you wake up, never complain that you are poor, think of those 86,400 seconds in your time account (which is the same amount as all the billionaires have). And invest those 86,400 seconds in things that matter. You cannot roll them forward to another day. The actions that you take today create your tomorrow.

Imagine If someone stole £100 or even £10 from you, you would be disappointed and go after them; but what about the people who are stealing your time by focusing on negativity and drama that is not serving you? The next time someone is stealing your time, think about it as them taking £1 from your time account for every one second you spend with them.

We will all hear negative things said to us and about us. It could only take 10 seconds to hear or read a comment that can destroy our day, week or even occupy our time for a longer period. View the comment that takes 10 seconds to hear as someone taking £10 from your time account and don't give them a penny more. Instead, switch back to the thought of how you are going to spend those valuable seconds now. How you spend your time today is what creates your tomorrow.

*"Invest Your Time Wisely Today In Order To Have A
Better Tomorrow."*
– Calum Kirkness

4. Level Of Property Knowledge

A lot of people make the mistake of thinking that they need to have a lot of knowledge to get started in property and allow their limiting belief to hold them back. The great thing about knowledge is that it can be learned. Your commitment and dedication will dictate the speed and level of knowledge that you will obtain.

How much property knowledge do you currently have?

The great thing about knowledge is that it can be learned relatively quickly. Once you have read and understood the complete Property Success Insider Formula, you will have more property knowledge than most others and be in a great position to jumpstart or scale your property investment and/or trading business.

Most people imagine that knowledge is the key to achieving success, which holds them back from getting started. They procrastinate and continue gathering more and more information and knowledge, leading to overwhelm and analysis paralysis. Whilst knowledge is very important, it is only part of the equation and there are other equally, if not more,, important things that you require in order to achieve success. These items will become apparent as you go through the book.

Knowledge is power but only if applied. If it is not going to be used, it may as well have never been learned in the first place.

> *"Action Without Knowledge Is Risky, Knowledge Without Action Is A Waste."*
> **– Calum Kirkness**

5. What Is Your Level Of Property Experience?

Knowledge is great but once it has been combined with experience, it becomes real.

When you are starting out, it is important to be honest and consider the level of property experience that you currently have:

No Experience

- Even if you feel that you have no property experience, you most likely do have some. We all live somewhere and have more than likely rented a room, apartment or house or maybe even bought our own house.

- Everyone must start from somewhere.

Some Property Experience

- Maybe you have a little experience and you are looking for more knowledge before exposing yourself to more.

Whatever your current position, I would encourage you to get started by taking some form of action, however small, that will increase your level of experience and knowledge today.

You don't need to be great to start anything. Make a decision to learn the basic knowledge and then make sure that you start in order to become great.

"Think Big - Start Small - Start Now."
– Calum Kirkness

6. Job or Investor?

Are you looking at property as a job or as an investor?

Do you have such a passion for property that you feel you would like to make it your job? Or do you see the property for the positive and safe passive income investment that it can provide?

The answer to this question will have a significant bearing on which property strategy you decide on.

Let's first look at property as a job. If you are committed to spending more than four hours per week on your property business, consider this as a job. A job in property may be for you if you enjoy deal making, working on and repairing property and dealing with tenants/guests.

If you are looking at property with a hands-off approach, where you want to spend less than four hours per week on your property business, then consider yourself a property investor. This is where you initially make your primary income from a different source and then invest your savings in property to provide a passive income to build your wealth. This is what many successful business people do, or people who have inherited some money and are looking for a safe investment.

7. Your Current Network

- Everyone has a network of people that they can tap into to varying degrees.
- Even if your network is not directly related to property, do not underestimate the value of it.
- Always start building your network before you need it.
- There is nothing more powerful than having the support of people to spread the word.

Your Network = Your Net Worth

We are the average of the top five people that we spend time with.

"You Should Always Build Your Network
Before You Need It."
– Calum Kirkness

10 Ways To Build Your Network:

1. Stay in touch with your local community.
2. Attend property network events.
3. Attend business networking events.
4. Visit the places where you are likely to find your ideal clients.
5. Visit places where you are likely to meet potential members for your power team.
6. Visit places where you are likely to meet potential joint venture partners.
7. Become the locally recognised expert in your field who attracts the right people.

8. Build an active online presence using social and professional media.
9. Always seek referrals.
10. Always follow up.

Some further tips to help:

- Use testimonials.
- Participate in industry meetings.
- Provide value by blogging, podcasts, etc.
- Be active in online forums.
- Be unconventional to be memorable.
- Join property-related social networking sites.

8. Location Where You Live

This is where you currently live and not necessarily where you will invest. They will ideally be the same or close together though.

Ideally you will live in an area that is a suitable prime location and goldmine area for you to invest and operate your chosen property strategy/business in. The closer you live to where you invest, the easier it becomes to manage and control your property investment business and cut down on costs, travel time, etc.

Important location factors to consider:

- Your property investment location must work for your strategy – cashflow, capital growth or both.
- It is ideally close to where you live. I would recommend this, particularly when you are starting out.
- If your prime location and goldmine area is located away from where you live, do you have a good team in place that you can trust and rely on?

We will go into the importance of investment location in more detail in the next chapter.

CHAPTER 5

SELECTING YOUR PRIME LOCATION AND GOLDMINE AREA

Selecting your prime location and goldmine area to invest in, is the single biggest and most important decision that you will make in building your property business and property investment portfolio, along with your preferred investment strategy.

They say that the three most important factors when you are investing in property are LOCATION, LOCATION, LOCATION. This is a true and important fact!

There are several factors which you should consider, and which will influence the selection of your prime location and gold mine area.

Before we go in to detail on the criteria, which will help you select your optimal prime location and goldmine area, I would like to share with you some basic principles and general rules of thumb that tend to occur in the property market.

- The higher the property value in the area, the lower the rental yield.
- The higher the potential for capital appreciation, the lower the potential for higher rental yield.

For example, the potential for capital appreciation in London was high for a period but the rental yields were relatively low. In contrast, the towns and cities in the north of England were achieving higher yields of 7 to 10+% but the potential for capital appreciation was low. In the last couple of years, property values in London have generally been falling, with the top end of the market being hit the hardest.

Key Factors To Consider In Selecting Your Prime Location And Goldmine Area:

- Population size of the town or city.
- Area/distance from where you live. Initially as close to where you live as possible or alternatively if you can move to the location that makes the best investment location.
- Population growth rate of the town or city.
- Employers, employment rate and opportunities in the town or city.
- Number of universities, colleges and schools and quality of education.
- The crime rates.
- The transport and infrastructure.
- The level and quality of amenities.
- The average income and range of incomes.
- The potential for capital growth.
- Is the location suited to cashflow strategies?
- Is the area under development/regeneration?
- Age demographics of the town or city.

It is important to focus on one prime location and goldmine area at a time, before adding additional areas.

Depending on the size of the town or city you select for your prime location and goldmine area, it could be just a small area of that town or city. Focus your attention on becoming the expert in that area and when you have done that, you will become the go-to person in that area and attract the best opportunities. Once you have mastered your area, you can gradually expand your property investment geographical area.

> *"Become The Expert In Your Prime Location And Goldmine Area."*
> **– Calum Kirkness**

In order to research and gain an in-depth knowledge of any location, there are some great sites and tools that you can find on the Internet to help you.

Researching the perfect prime location and goldmine area has never been easier.

The top property sites such as Rightmove, Zoopla, PrimeLocation, etc., are all great research sites and there are also some paid sites available. They all have their individual plus points and you can also research government sites for local and national statistics. I would advise that you set aside some time each day to look at these sites for your research, to identify and monitor trends and look out for new opportunities.

"With Your Budget, Always Look To Buy The Worst Houses In The Best Street Rather Than The Best House In The Worst Street."
– Calum Kirkness

"Property Is A Numbers Game. Know Your Numbers Inside Out And Base Your Decisions On Numbers Not Emotion."
– Calum Kirkness

"When Emotion Is High Intelligence Is Low."
– Calum Kirkness

CHAPTER 6

BUILDING YOUR POWER TEAM

You may have come across the term 'Power Team' before. It is a term used to describe a group of specialist experts that you regularly work with as part of your supply chain, and who you call on for advice, support, supplies and having work carried out. Your power team is an essential component of any successful property investment strategy and trading business, it should be specialised and a good match with your values, chosen strategy and location.

When building my power team or when I am considering additions or replacements, I have developed strategies to help me, based on models that have been tried, tested and proven to be effective. For example, when I am making power team decisions, I think about how a successful football club has been built up and how they succeed with certain managers and under-perform with others. I put myself in the position of the CEO, or manager, of a successful football club and ask myself: what would they do and how would they approach building up the key people in the club, in order that it becomes or remains the most successful?

A CEO of a football club wouldn't employ a rugby coach to manage the club, and a football manager wouldn't sign up a few new rugby players to play in the team. You get my point; your power team members need to be experts in your chosen property strategy and ideally in your chosen prime location and goldmine area.

Your Power Team Members:

- CEO – You.
- Manager – You.
- Coach or mentor?
- Deal finders (Sourcers).

- Legal advisor specialist in property.
- Finance specialist in property.
- Taxation specialist in property.
- Suppliers.
- Contractors.
- Tradespeople.
- Investors.
- Clients.

How To Find Members For Building Your Power Team:

- Google search.
- LinkedIn.
- Facebook.
- Property network events.
- General network events.
- Business functions.
- Social activities/hobbies.
- Advertising/signs.
- Private membership clubs.
- Recommendations/word of mouth.
- Always be alert and looking out, or listening, for people/companies being talked about or recommended. Opportunities to build and strengthen your power team are everywhere!
- Always carry business cards with you.

5 Key Things To Look For In Your Power Team

Your Power Team Members Should Be Engaged To Do The Things That:

- You can't do.
- You don't enjoy doing.
- They can do better than you.
- They can do quicker than you.
- Can be employed cheaper than the amount you can make by applying your time and expertise on other tasks.

Joint venture partners can also be considered as an important part of a power team.

There Are Four Crucial Elements To A Successful Joint Venture Partnership:

- The person or persons with the investment funds.
- The person or persons with the relevant knowledge.
- The person or persons with the relevant experience.
- The person or persons with the time.

It is very rare to find someone who has the investment funds, relevant experience, relevant knowledge and the time. When you can bring these people together, you can achieve much more than the individual parts and achieve a win-win for all partners.

It is important that the JV partners bring a balance of the above to the venture and that it is strong enough in all areas to maximise the chances of success.

The sum of the JV should be greater than the individual parts, otherwise you are better outsourcing the areas where you require support.

Always Consider:

- What value can you bring to the partnership?
- What would you like to get out of the partnership?
- Do you feel that all the other partners will benefit from the partnership?
- Can you work with all the partners in the joint venture?

Key Elements To Establish In Any Joint Venture Partnership:

- Number of parties.
- Purpose of JV.
- Contribution of each party.
- Structure.

- Valuation/split.
- Management/control.
- Talent resources.
- Contractual arrangements.
- Exit strategy and provisions.

Each of your service providers in your power team/JV partnerships should be performing at a high level of 80 out of 100%, or above, or you should be looking to replace them. It is also important to work with more than one service provider for each category if you can; this way, if one service provider lets you down, you are not left stuck. It also stimulates healthy competition to ensure efficient and competitive service.

Some of the team members will have little interaction with others and therefore it is not so important that they are a good fit with the other members of the team. Depending on how you structure your business, there may be some members of the team who will be required to work often, and interact closely, with others. You want to encourage your team to feel free to be creative and interact with other team members, so that you do not have to be relied on all the time for decisions. Be clear with what level of decision making you want to be included in and as time goes on, your team will begin to form relationships which everyone will understand. Create documented standards and systemise all common procedures.

When You Are Building Your Power Team:

- Look for nine or more people in each area of your power team.
- Select and interview six.
- Ideally add three of the best in each section if they are suitable and meet your criteria.
- Always aim to have three in all or most categories.

Replace any members who are consistently underperforming without delay, and always be looking to strengthen your powerteam.

8 Cs For Assessing And Building Your Power Team:

- **Competency** – They should be experts in the service that you are looking for.
- **Commitment** – They should be committed to providing a high level of service, if not look to replace them.
- **Collaboration** – They should be willing to collaborate with the team when required.
- **Culture** – Create a positive environment where team members can flourish.
- **Communication** – Make sure all communication is clear and avoids assumptions.
- **Creative** – Encourage creativity from the whole team.
- **Clarity** – Ensure that everyone is clear on the end goal and what is required from them.
- **Consequences** – Let the team members know that you are unable to accept poor performance, and this will lead to replacements being sought and appointed.

It is a good idea to review your power team regularly.

Building a strong and reliable power team takes time, but once you have it in place it makes your life as a property investor more efficient, more enjoyable and so much easier.

CHAPTER 7

UNDERSTANDING PROPERTY CYCLES

"Property Is Vanity - Equity And Profit Is Sanity -
Cashflow And Cash Is King."
– Calum Kirkness

An important and very useful tool of property investment is understanding that the property market has tended to follow cycles in the past. The cycle is referred to as the 18-year property cycle.

Once you understand the property cycle and the drivers behind it, you will be at an advantage to those who are either not aware of it or do not understand the factors behind it. Once you understand how the cycle works, you will know:

- The reason why property prices always rise over the long term, which provides confidence when investing that they will continue to do so in the future.
- That prices do not climb in a smooth linear upward trend, and there will always be dips during the cycle due to the way the system is set up and works.
- How the media operates and fuels the prices to rise beyond where they should and then decline lower than they would shoot beyond, without the dramatic attention-grabbing headlines that fuel human greed, panic and fear.

Once you are armed with the right knowledge, you can avoid making bad decisions at the wrong time that could potentially put your portfolio at risk. I would encourage you to include an understanding of property cycles as one of your central pillars of your investment knowledge. Sometimes it is better to do nothing and be patient in property, than to simply be doing deals for the sake of appearing being busy.

How you can use the 18-year property cycle to make better investment decisions.

Firstly, we need to have a look at the economics that underpin the cycles in order to understand why a property cycle has existed.

In almost every market, except for land, the forces of supply and demand help keep prices stable over time.

The land market is different because the amount of land that exists is fixed, except for a small amount of reclamation. This is the reason why I like land as an investment.

They Don't Make Any More Land

There are things that can be done to open more land for development, such as relaxing planning restrictions, but this is politically fraught and is the reason that it usually never happens in any great quantity or significance. Opening more areas of land also depends on the landowner's willingness to sell the land. Moreover, demand is normally concentrated around established locations, so not all land is appealing to developers.

When the economy is growing and there is a rising demand for new homes, shops and factories; this extra demand pushes prices to rise. Because there is no supply mechanism to control or pull prices back down, the land prices increase faster than wages and the price of goods. It doesn't take people long to realise what is happening and to see that they can achieve the best return on their money by investing in property, which is as a proxy for land, which is why I prefer freehold or commonhold apartments in Scotland than leasehold property.

At times of particularly high demand, which will be fuelled by the media and encouraged by the banks, people start speculating all over again by buying property on the assumption that the price will continue to go up. When property prices enter a phase where the prices are increasing faster than wages, they will eventually become unaffordable for most, and the boom phase comes to an end immediately followed by the bust phase.

When property prices plummet, causing chaos for the banks which have been lending money secured against the high-priced property, the banks withdraw lending and, in some cases, call in their loan. Building activity stops and businesses shut down, which all have a knock-on effect for the overall economy, stock markets and employment levels.

Eventually the property prices drop to a more sustainable level, everything begins to return to a normal level of activity and the property cycle starts to repeat itself all over again. Each cycle starts from a higher level than the previous one, which means that the long-term trend is always upwards.

The Different Stages Of The 18-Year Property Cycle

The economist, Fred Harrison, was one of the first people to identify that there was a property cycle which tended to follow a pattern of phases, each with typical durations.

It is best not to get overly concerned with the duration of each phase as they can vary. It is better to use the model as a guidance tool only when making investment decisions. It is also important to be aware of individual and macro-economic factors that can affect property prices in an individual town or city. For example, London property prices continued to rise post the 2008 financial crash, when most other areas fell. This was due to the rise of overseas investors buying properties in London. Prices in London began to decline in 2016. The property prices in Aberdeen, Scotland also continued to rise post 2008 due to the rising price of oil until 2014. When the price of oil declined, the property values in Aberdeen went into decline.

Most people will have a memory of at least one complete property cycle, possibly several. I have certainly witnessed two property cycles and I am now 48 years old. As I mentioned earlier in the book, when I was a teenager and first started working, inflation and interest rates were high (in the range of 15 to 20%), and saving interest rates were also sky high, (in double digit figures around 12 to 15%). If you wanted to borrow money, I think you were looking at 18%+.

As we talk about the indicators that signify each stage, you will most likely be able to look back and see some of the clues that were there in the past. It is important to understand how the property cycle works in order to be able to look for your own evidence.

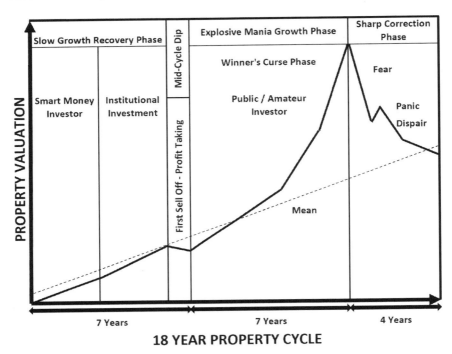

18 YEAR PROPERTY CYCLE

There Are Four Stages To Each Property Cycle:

At each stage of the cycle, the professionals who are watching the signals, act very differently from the amateurs who are watching the media and as a result make better investment decisions.

> *"A Professional Investor Watches For The Signals, An Amateur Watches And Follows The Media."*
> **– Calum Kirkness**

The best time to invest and buy property is when the amateur investor is selling due to fear and panic generated from the media and the public, and sell when there is mass optimism to buy amongst homeowners, buyers and the amateur investors.

When the media is creating a frenzy during rising house prices and others are rushing to buy, investors with the right knowledge and experience will, and should, be doing the opposite.

Phase 1: Slow Recovery – Preparing For The Party To Begin.

If we look at the cycle where prices have bottomed out at the end of the recession phase, and where the recovery phase is just beginning to get underway, this is the stage where the bravest and smartest investors get attracted back into the market. The market will generally overshoot in both directions, so this can be a good time to buy.

Investors get attracted back into the market by improved yields from the lower property prices, and rents tend to stay much the same, or fall by a lesser %, than property prices. This is because everyone still needs somewhere to live, and the population is still rising.

No one knows exactly at which point the bottom of the market has been reached, but smart investors are willing to take an educated guess, based on their knowledge that the upside potential outweighs the downside risk. They know it is only a matter of time before confidence returns to the market, the prices start to rise, and the cycle repeats itself.

Even if renters were feeling brave enough to take advantage of the lower house prices available at this stage, they are unlikely to be able to access finance as this is the toughest point in the cycle to get a mortgage.

Amateur investors are usually absent from the market at this stage, and those who are already invested might even panic sell at the bottom of the bust phase or be in a position where they are forced to sell because their portfolio and finances were poorly structured to weather a recession. This can be a phase when BMV deals are available, and purchase lease options are a solution for people who find themselves in negative equity.

If there is pessimism around, the media will be full of doom and gloom despite the major events of the recession seeming to be over and the recovery phase beginning to get underway. Remember: bad news sells much better than good news!

"Remember: Bad News, Which Is Designed To Create Fear
And Panic, Sells Much Better Than Good News!"
– Calum Kirkness

When You Understand The Principles, Use Them To Your Advantage!

As the recovery phase develops and more buyers have the confidence to enter the market, the effect is gradually rising property prices. A good indicator is to look out for big companies and pension funds starting to buy up distressed portfolios. They are the ones with the best market intelligence to know when it is time to buy; they cannot risk getting in too early.

In the early recovery phase, prime assets will always be the most attractive as the early growth tends to begin in the centres of the most economically powerful cities and then have a 'ripple out' effect from there. This effect in larger cities is another great way to profit from the property boom cycle phase. This is a strategy that requires an in-depth knowledge of the area and economic factors, which I cover in more detail in my property training events.

Phase 2: Slight Market Dip – Some People Drop Out Of Going To The Party.

Following the slow recovery in Phase One, there may be a slight mid-cycle dip as the earliest movers take their profits, and the recovery phase will begin to give way to the explosive phase.

Phase 3: Explosive Growth – The Party Is In Full Swing.

It is now clear that prices are increasing at a faster rate. The banks will have recovered and be over the shock and be more willing to lend again. As the house prices begin to increase faster than wages, the media will start to get interested and you will begin to see attention-grabbing headlines relating to house prices on a regular basis again. Public frenzy will start to get fuelled by the media headlines, and amateurs will start to speculate either by moving up the ladder to a bigger property before it gets even further out of their reach, or they will feel wealthy because of the increased equity in their home. Some will re-mortgage their home to release the equity and go on a buying spree to fund holidays and cars, etc. Banks start to make it easy for people to access money again and everything is back in full swing.

As momentum builds, logic and fundamentals once again go out of the window and group psychology kicks in. Everyone assumes that prices will keep going up, so they buy at any level pushing prices up even higher. Some of the smart investors who got in early with the knowledge of how this cycle works will quietly start preparing to sell off some, or all, of their properties to lock in their profits. If you have long-term property investment plans, it can be beneficial to hold on to your good performing properties even during a downturn. It takes time and money to both exit and re-enter the market, and there is also the lost rent during the time that you have sold a property. If you have any under-performing properties, now is the time to sell them.

As the cycle moves towards the peak of the explosive phase, it becomes a sellers' market and smart investors know it. Estate agents start conducting 'open house' style viewings to stoke demand even further, and properties that would have struggled to sell a few years earlier end up going to sealed bids and frequently sell for above their asking price. Developers start marketing 'off plan' properties to capitalise on the high demand.

Banks aren't immune to the mania either; they start to loosen up their lending criteria to grab a bigger piece of the action. You would expect banks to understand the property cycle and be more responsible with their lending. Here is the crazy part: even when some individuals within the banks are aware that the boom is unsustainable and likely to be coming to an end, they are still under pressure to compete with everyone else, and shareholders aren't happy to see them sitting back and not lending while everyone is so optimistic. There are also individual commissions and bonuses to consider. This lax credit approach keeps the party going on for longer than anyone would have previously expected.

At some point, a commentator or economist will predict that the party is about to end and everything is about to come crashing down because everything is so fundamentally overvalued. A year later, prices will still be rising "one for the road" style and that commentator/economist will be branded a "doom-monger". Mr Fred Harrison termed the final couple of years of the explosive phase the "winner's curse" phase. This is the time to offload any under performing properties or cash in if you wish to exit the market.

My worst performing property investment was an area of land that I purchased in 2006, which was at the beginning of the winner's curse phase. I paid more than the market value to secure the site due to its location and views and it was a site to build a house for myself so the decision was not based on numbers alone. It has still increased in value, just not as well as the land development investments made in 2001 at the start of the last explosive phase.

It is difficult to predict exactly when the final year of the explosive phase will occur until it has already happened, and by then it is too late to act. There will generally have been no shortage of warning signs to indicate that things are nearing the peak though.

Phase 4: Bust And Recession – The Party Is Over And The Hangover Sets In.

Because the market is being driven by sentiment rather than fundamentals in the boom years, it is easy for confidence to suddenly disappear and bring the market down with it. When this happens, prices drop and people who are over-leveraged are unable to afford to keep the property and go bankrupt, triggering waves of forced selling which pushes prices down even further. It is important to protect the downside so that you do not need to sell a property during this phase.

It is impossible to know exactly when this will happen, but you won't need to be told when it does. The media will fuel the panic with endless horror stories and remember that nothing grabs attention and sells better than bad news. Just like a hangover, the recession phase feels like it will last forever, but it never does and at some point, the smart money will be tempted back into the market and the whole cycle can start all over again.

How Can You Profit From The Property Cycle?

- Keep an eye on what the media headlines are saying.
- Understand whether it is a sellers' or buyers' market.
- Stockpile your cash and watch your LTV % during the winner's curse phase.
- Look to buy when the panic selling phase has bottomed out.
- Sell when others are in the manic buying phase, particularly any properties which have been under-performing in terms of cashflow.
- Avoid emotional buying and stick to the fundamentals.
- Avoid panic selling and stick to the fundamentals.
- Stick to investing in assets and avoid temptation to buy liabilities during the boom phase.
- Learn and understand global economic factors.
- Learn and understand micro and local economic factors for your investment areas.

The property cycle is a great tool to use as an indicator as to where the market may be at any given time, and more importantly where it may be heading.

"Winners Focus On Winning, Losers Focus On Winners."
– Calum Kirkness

"Leaders Anticipate, Losers React."
– Calum Kirkness

"Anticipation Is The Ultimate Power When It Comes To Succeeding."
– Calum Kirkness

Whilst it is never possible to accurately know what is going to happen next, understanding the property cycle will help you manage and reduce risk. It will also help you decide when to enter the market, how to prepare for a fall, which strategy to use when, and when to exit the market.

One final important point is to understand that you do not have to scrap the buy and hold strategy and start timing the market, although you can use this strategy if you want to. Due to the costs and time involved in selling a property, as well as the costs and time to get back into the market, some investors prefer to prepare themselves for the fall and hold their properties for the long term. When you consider the time, loss of income, costs, etc., this can all add up to the same as the decrease in value of the property.

If you stick to the very basic fundamentals described here, you have significantly increased your chances of doing very well in property investing.

CHAPTER 8

SELECTING THE RIGHT PROPERTY TYPE FOR YOUR STRATEGY

Selecting the right property type, condition and size are important considerations when it comes to compatibility with the property investment strategy and niche that you have selected.

Property Type

We Can Break Property Down In To Six Main Residential Property Types:

1. Studios.
2. Apartments.
3. Terraced houses.
4. Semi-detached houses.
5. Detached houses.
6. Commercial-to-residential opportunities.

Once you know what type of property to focus on for your strategy and goldmine area, it is important to consider the size of the property, the number of existing bedrooms and the number of potential bedrooms. The property strategy and niche market that you have selected will determine the number of bedrooms that you should focus on when buying property.

Once we know which type/size of property that we will focus on as part of our property business plan, there are 12 key items to consider when looking at the property:

1. Is it the right size and compatible with your property strategy?
2. Are you looking to purchase or control the property?
3. What is the ownership and title of the property or control agreement?

4.   What is the condition of the property?
5.   Is the property on the market and if so, for how long?
6.   How much work is required to be carried out on the property, and how much will it cost?
7.   How motivated is the owner to sell or lease the property?
8.   What is the EPC rating (Energy Performance Grade) of the property?
9.   Is the property occupied or vacant possession?
10. What is the asking price for sale or monthly lease?
11. What is the market value?
12. What is the RICS valuation of the property?

Property Ownership Types And Control Types

Ownership Types:

Freehold – This is my preferred ownership type for houses.

- Freehold = 100% ownership of the property:
- The freeholder of a property owns it outright, including the land that the property is built on.
- When you buy a freehold property, you are 100% responsible for maintaining your property and land, so you'll need to budget for these costs.

Leasehold

- Most flats and maisonettes are owned leasehold, apart from in Scotland where there are very few leasehold properties.
- Leasehold is where ownership of the property belongs to the buyer, but the land and common areas belong to the freeholder.
- The remaining lease period of the property is an important consideration, and the longer it is the better.
- Once the remaining lease period falls below 80 years, it can become problematic and typically should be avoided.
- The remaining lease period affects the value of the property. The

longer the lease, the higher the valuation.

- Leasehold can lead to problems between the leaseholder of the property and the freeholder of the land and common areas.
- Ground and maintenance payments are typically made to the freeholder monthly or annually.
- When you buy a leasehold property, you'll take over the lease from the previous owner. **Before making an offer, you'll need to consider 3 key things:**
    1. How many years are left on the lease?
    2. How will you budget for service charges and related costs?
    3. How will the length of the lease affect getting a mortgage on the property and the resale value?

Commonhold – This is my preferred ownership for apartments.

- Commonhold is where the property is owned freehold, and the common areas are owned and maintained between the owners of the properties within the building. This does away with some of the problems incurred in leasehold properties.
- The property owners appoint and have control of the maintenance providers and pay a monthly fee for this.
- There are no ground rents payable.

Property Control Types:

Purchase Lease Option

- The period of the lease option can vary up to a maximum period equal to the remaining period of the mortgage. Different investors tend to have different views on whether to keep the lease period short or keep it open for a longer period.
- This gives the right to buy, but not the obligation.

Rental Agreement:

- Also known as rent-to-rent

- Duration is typically two to five years.
- Gives control but not ownership or right to purchase the property.

Whether the property is to be purchased freehold, commonhold or leasehold or controlled via lease option or rental agreement, is an important consideration.

Condition of Property

Depending on which strategy you choose and the market conditions, this will determine whether the condition of the property is compatible with the strategy. When buying up existing property stock, the condition and level of work can be broken down into six main categories:

1. Walk-in condition.
2. Light refurbishment.
3. Minor refurbishment.
4. Major refurbishment.
5. Structural alterations.
6. Extending habitable area to add value.

When you are selecting the properties and looking at the level of work required to bring them up to walk-in condition, it is important to be realistic with your level of knowledge and experience. I encourage everyone to dream big and set their ambitions high, but also to be realistic and break the big dream down in to small manageable goals. If you are just starting out, get some experience with light refurbishment projects first and gradually increase the level of work required as your knowledge and experience grows.

A hard part of assessing the condition and work required to bring the property up to standard is costing the works. Most people under-estimate the cost of the works and the time involved, they therefore assess the maximum price that they can offer for the property too high. Due diligence and understanding the numbers is such an important factor and why there is a whole section in the book dedicated to it.

CHAPTER 9

DUE DILIGENCE

Due Diligence covers the process of investigation and verification of the details of a particular investment opportunity. It is extremely important to understand and carry out thorough due diligence on any investment opportunity and decision that you are considering. It is also important to stick to the fundamentals and not allow your emotions to cloud your key investment decisions. Allowing your emotions to cloud your judgement can seriously damage your wealth!

> *"When Emotions Are High, Intelligence Goes Down."*
> **– Calum Kirkness**

Before you have arrived at the stage of carrying out your due diligence on any particular property, it is important to know your prime location and goldmine area inside out, and have a good understanding of the property investment strategy that you have chosen to follow.

In selecting your property investment strategy, investment criteria and prime location and goldmine area, you have already carried out a large part of the due diligence process. It is now time to search for deals and carry out thorough due diligence on them to ensure that they meet your criteria and will make a good investment. Smart investing is all about minimising risk and maximising upside. Whilst it is never possible to eliminate all risk, your job is to minimise it as far as possible and due diligence will do that.

> *"Sometimes, The Best Investments Are The Ones That You*
> *Never Make At All."*
> **– Calum Kirkness**

When Setting Up Your Property Investment Business, There Are Four Key Areas Of Due Diligence To Cover:

1. Selecting the right property strategy that you would like to follow

and focus on – Due diligence for selecting your property strategy was covered earlier in the book. Your property strategy must be compatible with your character, strengths and goals and work in your prime location and goldmine area.

2. Selecting your prime location and goldmine area – Due diligence for selecting your property prime location and goldmine area was covered earlier in the book. Your prime location must be compatible with your property strategy and work for you logistically.

3. Selecting the right type, size and condition of property.

4. Assessing any potential deal fits with your property strategy and investment criteria.

You can see how each section of property investment links with the other and how one decision affects and leads to the next.

Your due diligence criteria will vary depending on which strategy you are focusing on. The numbers won't lie. Keep it simple. Stick to your criteria and if the deal stacks up, do it. If it doesn't, leave it.

Stick To The Fundamentals And Leave Emotion Out Of The Due Diligence Process.

The factors to be considered, researched and planned can be split into a number of key categories:

- Local market.
- Demographics.
- Economics.
- Property cycle.
- Location.
- Strategy.
- Property.
- Network and connectivity.
- Amenities.
- Convenience.

- Financial.
- Legal.
- Environmental and health.
- Planning.
- Misc.

Within each of these categories there are several individual checks which can, and should, be followed depending on your strategy.

The more you focus on your prime location and goldmine area, strategy, ideal customer, property type, size and condition, the easier and quicker the due diligence process becomes.

Always assess the deal with at least two exit strategies. For example, with a buy-to-flip deal, one of the criteria to assess the deal would be on the primary purpose of profit from the sell, but it is also important to consider the implications if the property doesn't sell. In this case, a good back up would be to ensure rental demand and prices in the area mean that the deal would also stack up as a buy-to-let property. By having two viable exit strategies, this reduces the risk.

Another example: back in 2007, the buy-to-flip strategy was working very well, buyer demand was high, property prices were climbing fast and everything looked great. But if you were in the middle of doing a buy-to-flip deal during the time when the market peaked and crashed, buyer demand disappeared quickly and property values dropped fast. If the developer had done their due diligence well, the chances are they would be able to still rent out the property and cover the costs of keeping it, rather than being taken out of the game and suffer losses, which was the case for many.

When Carrying Out Your Due Diligence, It Is A Good Idea To Split The Process Into Three Stages:

- Stage 1 – Free checks, which you can carry out online or by speaking to people who may have the knowledge.

- Stage 2 – Low cost checks – Physically visiting the property and low fee reports, etc.
- Stage 3 – Higher cost checks – Professional Surveys, checks and reports should only be carried out if your initial due diligence indicates that the deal stacks up.

There is no point in spending money on any due diligence checks if the deal does not stack up under the free checks that you can carry out.

Only move to the next stage of the due diligence process when the deal stacks up in the previous stage.

Whilst it is important to carry out thorough due diligence, it is equally important not to over analyse and let analysis paralysis take you out of the game.

CHAPTER 10

NEGOTIATING THE DEALS

Negotiation skills to get you the best deals and win-win outcomes:

Negotiation is the process where two or more parties come together with different needs to find a solution that is acceptable to all.

Negotiation is an essential skill in property investment. It forms a significant part in the level of success that you may achieve in property and the rate at which you will achieve it.

Negotiation Is Required To:

- Build your power team.
- Find opportunities.
- Get the best prices and the terms.
- Negotiate finance, rental rates or selling prices.
- Get the best prices from builders, suppliers, etc.

You can see how much of a role negotiation plays in building a successful property business. It is well worth studying, and practicing, your negotiating techniques.

As a starter, I have listed 10 negotiation techniques below:

1. Prepare, prepare, prepare

By failing to prepare, you are prepared to fail. Make sure you have done your research and understand the needs of the other party, or parties, to the negotiation. Always be clear on what you want out of the negotiation. Researching the other side to get a better understanding of their needs, as well as understanding their strengths and weaknesses, will put you in the best position to achieve the desired outcome. Negotiation is about mediating the best outcome for all involved and building long-term relationships based on trust and win-win outcomes.

2. Timing

Timing is important in any negotiation. You must know what to ask for, but also be sensitive and know *when* to ask for it. There are times when it is appropriate to press ahead and times when it is best to wait. When you feel at your best and strongest during the negotiations, this is the best time to ask for what you want. Be aware of not pushing ahead too hard though and damaging the negotiations.

3. Leave your ego out of the negotiations

The best negotiators are the ones who are detached from the outcome and don't care, or don't *show* they care, about the result or about who will get the credit for a negotiating a successful deal. Good negotiation is about making the other side feel like the final agreement was all *their* idea.

4. Listen more, talk less

The best negotiators are often the ones with the best listening skills. We have two ears and one mouth, use them in this ratio and spend twice as much time listening as talking! The best negotiators encourage the other side to talk first and patiently listen whilst others make their case. It is generally better to let the other side go first. Even if they don't mention numbers, it gives you a chance to ask what they are thinking.

5. Ask for what you want

Successful negotiators are assertive, challenge everything and know that everything is negotiable. Being assertive means asking for what you want in a polite manner and refusing to take an offer that does not meet your criteria.

It is important to note that there is a big difference between being assertive and being arrogant and/or aggressive. Being assertive means taking care of your own interests and emotions, whilst maintaining respect for the interests of other parties.

You must be able to make up your own mind, as opposed to believing everything that you are told. On a practical level, this means you have the right to question everything you are told.

6. Anticipate compromise

In any negotiations, you should expect, plan and be prepared to compromise and make concessions. The other side will more than likely be thinking the same. Every buyer wants to feel that they have got a good deal, and every seller wants to feel they drove a hard bargain.

7. Offer and expect commitment

There is quite often conflicting advice when it comes to who makes the first offer. Some will tell you to never make the first offer, others will tell you to make it. I think it depends on the situation. If the other party makes the first offer, it gives you an indication to where the negotiations may go, but never accept their first offer, even if it is what you were hoping for. You never know what else you might be able to negotiate, and you can always come back to the original offer which they have made. If you are making the first offer when buying, start low. Your first offer should feel uncomfortable; if it's not, it's too high. If you are selling, avoid being too ambitious or greedy, which could result in the other party walking away.

You should offer commitment from your side to bringing about the best outcome so you comfort the other parties. Avoid deals where the other side does not demonstrate the level of commitment that you would expect. If it doesn't feel right, the chances are it isn't right. Trust your intuition and be prepared to do what is necessary to demonstrate your commitment to a deal, but also be ready to walk away.

8. Their problems are their problems

In most negotiations, the other party will want you to hear all about their problems and for their problems to become your problems. Avoid this and deal with each individual issue as it comes up and try to find solutions.

9. Stick to your principles

As an individual and professional property investor, you should develop a set of guiding principles and values that you are not prepared to compromise on during any negotiation. If you find negotiations crossing your boundaries, don't be afraid to walk away.

10. Patience

Sometimes the timing is not quite right in order to be able to negotiate a deal within the boundaries of what is required to make a viable deal. Be prepared to walk away but keep the door open. When you are dealing with motivated sellers, there are different levels of motivation, and if they do not get a deal with someone else then quite often the deal will come back to you. When this happens, you are now in a stronger position to negotiate a deal which meets your criteria and stacks up. Remember what I shared with you about the farmer who came back to me a few times asking to buy my house before I finally agreed to sell.

Example And Case Study Of Negotiating For What You Want:

One nice Sunday in 2011, whilst I was working away from home with little to do on this day, I decided that I would go for a drive around the countryside and explore some new places. Everywhere I go, construction and new home signs are always attracting my attention, even when I am on holiday! As I mentioned in the beginning of the book, construction and property is in my DNA and I have been exposed to it since I could first see, hear and walk. I am always looking around for new ideas and to see what is happening in the industry. When I followed the signs on this day, I came across a new housing development. My initial impression was that it was a very nice development with good potential. It looked like a lot of effort had gone in to the design, so I went in to look around and ended up in the marketing suite, simply because I had time to spare and was curious. I was shown the model for the development and taken on a tour of the show homes, which were presented very nicely. The sales representative advised me which plots with the same or similar homes were currently available in the development. I saw there was potential here for getting in on a development in the early stages. Some will tell you never to buy new property, and it is certainly true that you need to be careful and know what you are doing. I have successfully bought brand new property and also purchased off-plan property, which have performed well.

My position at the time was that I was ready to start investing again and open to expanding my buy-to-let property portfolio, but not in any rush. The deal needed to be right. Think back to the property cycle model that I shared earlier in the book. The peak of the market had been in 2008, house prices had been falling significantly for the last few years and were now showing signs of bottoming out. It was looking like a good time to start buying again. Confidence for home buying was still low with the general public, the media was doom and gloom on property. Remember Warren Buffett's advice about buying when others are fearful and selling when others are greedy.

Following my visit to the development, I left and spent the next couple of hours driving around the area to see what was going on and get a feel for it. This is a great way to carry out your initial due diligence in an area. Then over the next few days, I carried out some online research on the area.

During the coming week, I received follow-up calls from the sales consultant to see what I was thinking. I mentioned to the sales consultant that I would be interested in purchasing the show homes, but not any of the other properties. She advised that she didn't think that would be possible, but would speak to the developer. It would be a stupid decision for the developer to sell the show homes at that stage of the development as the properties offered the best location and it would some time before replacement show homes were ready. If people can view and experience the property, their chance of buying increases, but that was my criteria if I was going to invest in the development.

I stuck to my position and made them an offer for the show homes, which was below the asking price. They advised that my offer was too low and proceeded to make some counter proposals, none of which met my criteria. Over the coming weeks, I continued to receive calls from the sales consultant and each time I stuck to my original proposal and offer. But guess what? Soon after, my offer was accepted.

When you think back to the other chapters and lessons in the book, there are several key lessons that come together and can be learned from this example.

CHAPTER 11

FUNDING YOUR PROPERTY INVESTMENT BUSINESS AND DEALS

When it comes to finance and borrowing money, it is important to understand that there are two different types of debt. Your mindset will dictate whether you view debt with a Good debt "Rich Dad" or Bad debt "Poor Dad" mentality.

Robert Kiyosaki's book *Rich Dad Poor Dad* is a great read in understanding good and bad debt.

- **Good debt** – Makes you more money than it costs you. It is where you invest in an asset that makes more money than the sum required to pay the finance payments and other costs relating to it. Property is a great example of where finance is normally good debt, providing you carry out your due diligence correctly and the numbers stack up. When you think of good debt, think of assets, cashflow and profit.
- **Bad debt** – Is where you take on finance to spend on goods or items which provide little or no return, and the return is less than required to cover the finance payments. This is known as a liability and loss. For example, a car is an example of a liability, unless you are a taxi driver or you have a strategy where you can charge for the use of the car. When you think of bad debt, think of liabilities and loss.

Another important concept to understand in property investment is leverage. Leverage is what makes property such a great asset class. When investing in property, a bank will generally lend you 75% of the purchase price or market value, whichever is lower in the form of a mortgage (subject to meeting their lending criteria), which means you need 25% deposit to complete the deal, plus expenses. So, you get 100% of the benefit for 25% of the input.

A great illustration of how property is viewed as one of the safest investments, is when you go to a bank and they will lend you 75% of the value of the property if you have 25% deposit, but they wouldn't lend you money to buy shares in their own bank.

As we have seen in the property cycle section of the book, pre-2008, it was easy for people to obtain finance to purchase property, and you could typically get an 85% LTV BTL mortgage (or even higher LTV) if the property was for your main residence. Property values were climbing fast, so even if you bought at market value at the time, it wasn't too long before you could refinance and get your next deposit to purchase your next property. Some investors who were buying BMV were re-mortgaging the same day, to have money in their pocket. This was how many people managed to build up a property portfolio so quickly pre-2008. The rules have since changed and you have to wait six months before being able to re-mortgage now.

The stumbling block for many now to get started buying investment property or to add to their property portfolio, is obtaining the mortgage and the deposit.

Post-2008, when bank lending changed significantly and tightened up, several new creative ways of financing deals have developed and materialized which help both the lender and the borrower. With low savings interest rates being offered by the banks, which were and typically still below the rate of inflation, this meant that anyone sitting with funds in the bank was more than likely seeing the value of their money being eroded away. As a property investor with the right knowledge, you can offer these savers/investors an attractive return on their investment, creating a win-win situation.

Examples Of Where You Can Or Maybe Able To Access Your Own Funds To Invest In Property:

- Your cash savings.
- Release equity in your own home.

- Cash in investments – stocks, shares, ISA, commodities.
- Your pension fund/s.
- Reduce outgoings to increase the rate your savings grow.
- Sell items you no longer require.

It is important to understand good and bad debt, and the advantages and disadvantages of each different source. You should always obtain professional financial and tax advice to determine the most appropriate and beneficial means and ensure that you are aware of the risks.

Things You Need To Know About Raising Investment Capital The First Time Around:

- Raising capital is about building relationships.
- People invest in business models, strategies and people, not ideas.
- Investors exist at all levels of sophistication.
- There are investors with cash to invest, and there are investors with cash and specific strategic knowledge to invest.
- Investors are everywhere.
- Think about the term of investment.
- Keep in mind that your idea is only new to you.
- Offer a clear, confident, concise pitch with certainty.
- Always check the terms and conditions and have signed legally binding agreements.

Examples Of Ways To Access Other People's Money (Private Funding):

- Family.
- Friends.
- Network.
- Investors.
- Crowd-funding.
- Joint ventures.

Some Funding Options From Financial Institutions:

- BTL Mortgage.

- Commercial funding.
- Bridging finance.
- Secured or unsecured loan.
- Credit cards.

When accessing mortgages or loans from financial institutions, there is a wide and varied range of options. It is important to understand these options and know which product will best fit your needs. This is where building a good relationship with bank managers and brokers can be valuable in forming your power team.

Let's have a quick look at some of the things to consider when selecting the best funding option:

- Choosing interest-only mortgage vs. capital repayment mortgage. Interest only is the most common for property investment as it increases monthly cashflow.
- Is the funding interest rate fixed or variable rate?
- There may be a discounted product for example where the first two years are at a discounted rate, after which the interest rate transfers to a standard variable rate.
- Arrangement fees.
- Early repayment penalties. These can be substantial and something to look out for if you plan to re-mortgage within the first few years.
- Completion fees.
- Any other misc. fees.

Credit Score

It is always a good idea to keep an eye on your credit score and profile to check that it is accurate and up to date. If there is anything adverse on your credit report, it is worthwhile checking to see if it can be removed. Always aim to keep your credit report clean by paying your bills on time and keeping your debt low.

A good credit score is a big plus in terms of accessing finance. If your credit report and score are not so good, you can still succeed in property by accessing private finance from family, friends, your colleagues and network, private investors, joint venture partners, etc.

Why Should Anyone Give You Any Money?

When You Are Looking To Attract Investment Funds From Investors, Which Is Not Easy, It Is Possible If You Have The Following Three Things:

1. You Need A Project

- What is the project that you want to do?
- Why do you want to do it?
- You need to be able to have a story to tell about your project.
- Is it worthwhile for other people to get involved in?
- Is it interesting to other people?

2. You Need An Audience

- You need to have people to tell your story to.
- Target your ideal investor.
- The larger your audience, the more potential money you can raise.
- This is where you can use the power of public speaking to speak one to many rather than one to one. As a trained speaker myself, I include a section in my property training programmes designed to help you with this.

3. You Need An Offer

- You need to have a clear offer and a call to action.
- Where's the urgency?
- Why should your audience act now?
- What will they get in return and when?
- Your offer needs to be clear in what you're asking for?

Approach the process in the same way as if you were looking to attract a long-term life partner. Not everyone you meet will be a suitable investor.

Don't appear desperate or try to rush the process. Making a marriage proposal on a first date rarely results in a "yes" and if it did, the chances are that it would end in disaster! The same is true when seeking funding partners.

"Make Yourself An Appealing Investment Prospect."
– Calum Kirkness

"First Impressions Matter, You Don't Get A Second Chance To Make A First Impression."
– Calum Kirkness

"Whilst First Impressions May Get You In The Door, Your Knowledge And Track Record Will Keep The Door Open."
– Calum Kirkness

First you need to make yourself visible and appealing to potential investment partners. They need to know that you exist, and you need to fish in a pond where the type of people that you wish to attract swim. i.e. people with money to invest.

Make yourself visible, known and respected both online and offline.

You need to be crystal clear in what you have to offer your potential investor in return for them funding your deals.

The sequence in attracting investors is the same as in dating. Each stage takes a little more time and investment than the previous stage.

- Step 1 – Obtain the telephone number or exchange a message. Free.
- Step 2 – Invitation for coffee. Low cost.
- Step 3 – Invitation for lunch or dinner. Low cost.
- Step 4 – Invitation to event or business weekend getaway. Medium cost.

- Step 5 – Proposal – When you feel comfortable with the relationship, make your investment proposal.
- Step 6 – Receive yes or no If you receive a yes, proceed to have legal agreement drawn up.

These are the key criteria that you will generally need to meet in order to obtain a yes from an investor. They need to:

- Know you.
- Like you.
- Trust you.
- Respect you.
- Understand your proposal (if you confuse them, you lose them!)
- Know what they will get in return (Make it a win-win).
- Always ensure that your credit score is the best that it can be.

Mastering the skill of raising finance will give you a massive advantage in the world of property and success. When you have access to unlimited funds, you can complete an unlimited amount of the best deals and achieve a high level of success.

CHAPTER 12

REGULATIONS, PERMISSIONS, PROTECTION

If you want to be wealthy, you not only need to know how to make money and build wealth, but you also need to understand how to protect and keep it. It is important to understand how you can do this by legally minimising the amount of tax that you pay, protecting the downside with the relevant insurances and ensuring you are operating in compliance with all the rules and regulations to avoid any penalties and fines.

In property investment and trading there are many rules and regulations to comply with, and a number of licenses and permissions which may be required. Then there are insurances, some of which are mandatory, some highly recommended and others desirable but not essential.

There are a lot of people in the property investment sector who are operating in a manner that is non-compliant. Sometimes this is due to lack of knowledge and awareness, and this is where it is important to have a specialist power team in place to keep you advised and compliant.

Failure to comply with these rules, regulations and insurances can be costly and lead to criminal charges, fines, delays to selling property and other significant costs and problems.

As you build up your property investment and/or trading business, it is important to adopt a wealth mindset and protect your interests and assets.

This chapter looks at the main elements permissions and protections and how to protect your wealth.

Six Key Elements Of Permissions and Protections:

1. Ownership/control.
2. Planning permission compliance.
3. Building regulations compliance.

4. Licences/registration/data protection.
5. Lenders consent.
6. Protection/insurances.

Ownership Titles

If you are purchasing a property, it is important to have the legal title registered with the Land Registry System. This will be handled by the legal conveyancing solicitor as part of the buying process. It is important to be aware and understand any, and all, legal aspects of the property title and any restrictions.

Control Agreements

If you are controlling a property, it is important to consider the agreement type and have it legally prepared as a binding agreement between parties.

Planning Compliance/Application/Approvals

Planning regulations are a complex area. Some people make the mistake of not taking expert advice or attempting to evade the system and carry out works which require permission – only to find out later when the authority notice, or the works are reported by a neighbour or someone else or when they come to sell the property. Getting planning permission wrong can be a costly mistake and lead to the works being demolished, or a lengthy process of getting the permissions to keep the works in place and a lost or delayed sale of the property.

Planning Process

- Do not make any assumptions when it comes to planning regulations, as any wrong assumptions can prove costly.
- Always check with an experienced local planning consultant or direct with your local planning department to see if planning consent would be required for any change of use or alterations to the property that you would like to make.

- A good resource for making preliminary checks in England regarding planning can be found at: https://www.planningportal.co.uk/info/200125/do_you_need_per mission.
- If planning permission is required for your planned project, then a planning application will be required. This will need to be prepared and made by someone who is suitably qualified and approved to make such applications. There will be an application fee which must be made with the application. The fees are generally available on the local authority website.
- Once a planning application has been lodged, it will be acknowledged as complete or incomplete. If incomplete, the missing information will need to be submitted before the application is fully accepted. After this, they will decide if it will be accepted, accepted with conditions, or rejected.
- Your local planning department will have a specified period in which to determine your application. If they require more time for any reason, then they will write to you explaining the reasons why.
- Sometimes the planning process is not easy.

Going back several years now, I submitted a planning application to build eight apartments on a brownfield development site that I had purchased. The application received objections from the surrounding neighbours. As the neighbours had submitted objections, it meant that the application would have to go to the planning committee, which is made up of local councillors who are not specialists or experts in planning to decide the application. As part of the planning process, I worked with the planning officer dealing with the application to make several amendments until they were in a position where they felt the application was suitable. The application report was submitted to the planning committee by the planning officers recommending approval. Despite the planning officers recommending approval, the planning application was rejected by the planning committee.

The location of the site meant that the neighbouring properties on one side of the road were represented by one councillor and the residents on the other side of the road were represented by another, which meant that the neighbours had two councillors to lobby increasing their chances of the committee voting against the application.

Everyone wants development but no one wants development in their back yard. This is known as 'NIMBY' in the property world (short for 'Not in My Back Yard').

The outcome of the planning process can be political with it coming down to a case of *who* you know rather than *what* you know.

If your strategy is a new-build property or extension and changes to an existing property and you are looking to flip the property for profit, an important factor to consider when you are designing the scheme is how contentious it may be for neighbours and the planning officers, as it could slow down the process. When you are looking to flip the property for profit, it can sometimes be best to be less ambitious with the application for speed. Time = Money.

All or most property investors and developers will have stories to tell on planning. Eg. Throughout my 20+ years of property investment, I've discovered time and again that planning is not always a level playing field.

Building Regulations Compliance/Applications/Approval

The building control process is less subjective than the planning process. There is a set of Building Regulations Standards which must be complied with and it is important to understand whether the works that you intend carrying out to a property will require Building Control approval or not. If the works require approval, then an application must be made and approval provided before the works commence. With building regulations and building control approval, it is a matter of either complying and getting Building Control Approval or not. There can still be grey areas and different interpretations in the process, but it is not a political process like planning can be.

The Different Stages Of Building Regulations Process To Understand:

- Functions of Building Control
- What are the Building Regulations?
- Building Control Applications
- Building Control Inspections
- How to book a Building Control Inspection
- Building Control Completion Certification

Functions Of Building Control:

- The main functions of the Building Regulations are to ensure the health and safety of people in and around buildings by ensuring that the building design and construction meet at least the minimum requirements and standards.
- With an increasing emphasis on environmental protection and conservation of energy, one role of Building Control is to encourage the innovation to produce more energy efficient and sustainable buildings. Buildings are now given an energy performance rating known as EPC which is short for Energy Performance Certificate. The rating lets the building owner or occupiers know how energy efficient the building is. The greater the energy efficiency of the building, the more cost efficient it is to maintain. This can be an important factor in determining the monthly rental price and attractiveness of your property to tenants or guests and also the sale price and salability of the property.
- The Building Regulations Standards are extensive, and part of the Local Authority Building Control Officers role is to educate and inform building professionals, contractors and trades people on meeting the regulations.
- Drive out rogue traders. Unfortunately, rogue traders still exist and there are still people who employ them. Having good and reliable builders as part of your power team is important to the success of property investment and development.

- Enhance access for disabled, sick, young and old people through having level access to buildings, level access showers, wider door openings, heights of fittings, automated doors, etc.
- Protect the community from dangerous structures. If buildings suffer structural damage or are poorly maintained, they can pose a danger to the public. Building Control will contact the owner to get the building made safe or if the building owner fails to carryout measures to make the building safe, the Local Authority can do it and pass the costs to the owner.
- Provide advice in support of the emergency services. Building Control can assist the emergency services in assessing whether a building is safe to enter, etc
- Ensure sports grounds and public venues are safe for crowds. I am sure you will agree that it is important to feel safe when attending events, particularly large events where structural loading is high and fire safety and means of escape in the event of an emergency is crucial.

What Are The Building Regulations?

- The Building Regulations are made up of Approved Documents which offer guidance on how to comply with the regulations, which are there to protect the occupants of the property, members of the public and the environment. The approved documents and standards vary between each part of the UK. and the approved documents for England, Scotland & Northern Ireland can be found using the links below.
  https://www.gov.uk/government/collections/approved-documents
  https://www.gov.scot/policies/building-standards/monitoring-improving-building-regulations/
  http://www.buildingcontrol-ni.com/regulations/technical-booklets
- The Approved Documents for Wales, didn't appear to be available online or working at the time of publication:

- For self-builders and renovators in England, the Planning Portal, offers advice on how to get approval as well as up-to-date versions of the Approved Documents which you can access using the following link:

  https://www.planningportal.co.uk/info/200128/building_control

- It is the responsibility of those carrying out the work to ensure that the provisions of the regulations are fully met. The role of Building Control is only to check that works have been carried out to comply with the regulations.

Building Control Applications

- There are different types of applications, depending on the nature of the work and the area where the works are being carried out.
- The first thing to determine is if you require building regulations approval? An independent expert or the building control department at your local authority will be able to advise you. Once you know whether the works require building control approval or not, the application type and route can be decided and followed if required.
- Most building work whether new, alterations, extensions or change of use – require building regulations approval.
- It is important to note that even though your proposed works may be exempt from the building regulations, you may still be required to obtain planning permission. You can gain accurate and up-to-date information from your local authority planning department or an independent planning expert.
- It is best to make the application online – Most, if not all, local authorities have the facility to apply online and in the modern age, I think this is the best and most efficient way to submit, manage and track your application.
- You can also make an application by post or by hand.
- There are fees associated with making an application, which must be made at the same time as the application. The fee will vary depending on the nature of the application and cost of the works.

Building Control Inspections

There are generally up to nine mandatory inspections, however not all nine are relevant to some jobs. Please note that all the relevant stages of work applicable to the job must be provided, these are:

- Commencement.
- Excavation for foundations.
- Foundations constructed, e.g. concrete poured.
- Damp proof course laid.
- Oversite ready for concreting.
- Structural members.
- Drains laid and visible.
- Drains testing.
- Completion.

It is common for more than one inspection to be carried out on one visit.

As well as these mandatory inspections, further inspections may also be necessary, as some jobs will require specific inspections such as fire protection and the reinforcement of concrete structures. In addition, a building control officer may call unexpectedly at other times to check on the work as it progresses. Building up a rapport with your local building control officer and doing what is required and having the works ready for inspection when you have arranged an inspection is an important part of the process.

It is a good idea to take plenty of photographs of the works as they proceed, particularly works which are to be covered up.

How To Book An Inspection?

- To book a building control inspection, you can call your local building control department to advise which stage is required to be inspected and make an appointment with the building control inspector for the area to visit your project.
- Inspections will be carried out after notice has been given. It is

therefore critical to provide the notifications and stick to the dates to ensure no delay to the works.

- Inspections can normally be arranged with just a few days' notice.

Building Control Completion Certification

- Once the works have been completed and signed off by the building control officer, a completion certificate will be issued for the works by the Building Control Department within the Local Authority. It is important to have the completion certificate in place for legal occupation of the space and any future sale of the property. Failure to have the completion certificate for the works can delay any future sale of the property.

What Is The Difference Between Planning And Building Control?

A lot of newbie property investors and traders get confused with the difference between planning permission and building control:

- Most people entering the property investment and development sector, generally realised that some form of permission is required for building work or alterations to be carried out to properties. However, the difference between obtaining planning permission and building regulations approval may not always be clear and some make the mistake of thinking they do not require them or only require one or the other. Making assumptions or mistakes in this area can prove to be costly.
- Building regulations set the standards for the design and construction of buildings to ensure the health and safety of the people in, or around, those buildings. The major items are the structural stability of the building to ensure the building or parts of it will not collapse or a section of it become loose or detached causing a hazard, the drainage systems to ensure the environmental health of those in and around the building are protected and the risk of flooding is prevented. They also include requirements to ensure the safety of the electrical installation, the energy efficiency of the building to conserve fuel and power and

that facilities are provided for people, including those with disabilities, to access and move around inside the buildings. Eg ramps leading to doorways, level access thresholds at doorways, level access showers, wider door openings, heights of ironmongery, etc.

- Planning is designed to guide the way towns, cities and the countryside develop. This includes the use of land and buildings, the appearance of buildings, landscaping considerations, highway access and the impact that the development will have on the general surrounding environment.
- For many types of building work, separate permission under both planning and building control will be required. For other building work, such as internal alterations, buildings regulations approval will probably be needed, but planning permission may not be.
- It is important to note that you may also have duties and responsibilities under the construction health and safety regulations.

Licences, Registrations And Data Protection

When you are operating a property investment or trading business, there will be licences, registrations and data protection to consider, which will vary depending on your property investment and trading strategies.

Here Are Some Of The Main Ones That Need To Be Considered:

Landlord Registration

- Landlord registration is designed to protect tenants from bad (or 'rogue') landlords.
- There is no registration scheme as such, only the three different types of licensing that operate across the UK.
- They all maintain up-to-date information about private landlords and their properties.
- They are used to make sure that tenants won't have to put up with poor quality or unsafe housing.

HMO Licence

Mandatory HMO Licencing

- These regulations are changing and getting tighter. You should always contact your local authority to find out what regulations apply in the area you are considering operating in. Different areas have different criteria.
- Selective licensing zones were introduced to deal with problems of poor property management and anti-social behaviour (ASB).
- All privately-rented properties within a selective licensing zone must be licensed, regardless of their occupation and size. Landlords without a licence may be prosecuted and may no longer be able to operate their business.

Additional licence

- If you operate a house in multiple occupation that is shared by three of more tenants living in two or more households. This excludes houses in multiple occupation that require a mandatory licence.
- If you wish to operate a house as an HMO, it must have the correct class of planning use. You may need to apply for planning permission to change it to the correct planning class.
- There is no guarantee that your planning application will be approved, but if you rent out your property you must have a property licence. If you are refused planning permission for an HMO, they are unlikely to refund your licensing fee.

Property Ombudsman

Benefits of joining the scheme:

- Membership of The Property Ombudsman (TPO) demonstrates your commitment to professional standards.
- Increases consumer confidence.
- Develops staff knowledge and service standards.
- Saves you and your customer legal fees and time.

- Enables you to concentrate on your business.

Deposit Protection

- All tenant deposits must be placed in a tenancy deposit protection (TDP) scheme if you rent out your home on an assured shorthold tenancy that started after 6th April 2007.
- These government-backed schemes ensure your tenants will get their deposit back if they:
  - Meet the terms of your tenancy agreement.
  - Don't damage the property.
  - Pay the rent and bills
- You (or your letting agent) must put your tenants' deposit in the scheme within 30 days of getting it.
- Available schemes – You can use any of the following schemes if your property is in England or Wales:
  - Deposit Protection Service.
  - MyDeposits.
  - Tenancy Deposit Scheme.
- There are separate TDP schemes in Scotland and Northern Ireland.
- All TDP schemes offer you two options:
  1. The scheme holds the deposit for free – known as a 'custodial' scheme.
  2. You or the agent holds the deposit and you pay the scheme to insure it – known as an 'insured' scheme.
- At the end of the tenancy:
  - The deposit must be returned to your tenants within 10 days of you both agreeing how much they'll get back.
- If you're in a dispute with your tenants:
  - The deposit is protected in the scheme until the issue is settled.
  - If you're in an 'insured' scheme, you or the agent must give the deposit to the TDP scheme. They will hold it until the issue is settled.

Data Protection

Data protection has been big in the news recently, due to large leaks of personal data by some large organisations. People are rightly becoming more and more sensitive to how their personal data is stored, used and secured.

As a property investor, if you are handling people's personal information, then it is important that you have compliance measures in place:

- The Data Protection Act 1998 requires every organisation, sole trader who is processing personal data to comply with the legislation.
- If you are not sure if you need to register, you can check online at: https://ico.org.uk/for-organisations/register/

Client Account

- A client account is an account at a bank in the name of the company to which it has been sent, but is separate from all other accounts linked to that company.
- If you receive or hold clients' money, then you must do so in accordance with the Clients' Money Regulations, 2012. For example, if you are a property sourcer or deal packager and receive a deposit or reservation fee from your clients, you must use a client account to hold the monies in.

Insurances

There are a range of insurances which you either must have, or at least consider having when you are investing in property.

8 main insurances which you either must or should consider having:

Landlord Insurance (must have depending on strategy)

- Landlord insurance can be tailored to cover you for the things that you feel are most important such as:
    - Building insurance.
    - Landlord's content insurance.
    - Legal protection.
    - Loss of rent insurance.

Buildings & Contents Insurance (should have)

- Whilst this type of insurance is not compulsory, if you own property it makes sense to protect it with at least the basic cover for fire and flood, and it also includes coverage for the fixtures and fittings.
- If you work from home don't forget that some domestic building and contents policies will not provide cover for the running of a business from home, so it is always best to check with your provider if you are covered and, if not, to take out the extra cover as required.

Professional Indemnity Insurance (PI) (should have depending on strategy)

- This insurance, whilst not being required by law, covers your legal liability for any advice that you provide in a professional capacity. It also covers you for liability of breach of professional duty in relation to any service that you provide in exchange for a fee.

Public Liability Insurance (could have)

- This type of insurance is not required by law but covers you against the risk of death, injury or damage at the property suffered by a third-party, including members of the general public or any other business that work with you.

- If in the process of providing your service, you meet members of the public or work with other businesses, it is worth considering obtaining suitable cover.

Employers' Liability Insurance (must have – if requirement met)

- This insurance is required by law if you employ anyone directly, and covers you if that employee were to fall ill or get injured as a result of the work they carry out for you.

Income Protection Insurance (could have)

Income protection insurance is designed to help you if you are unable to work if you are ill or injured, and ensures that you continue to receive a regular income until you retire or are unable to return to work. It will generally:

- **Replace part of your income** – if you can't work because you become ill or disabled.
- **Pay out until you can start working again** – or until you retire, die, or the end of the policy term – whichever is sooner.
- **There is often a waiting period before the payments start** – you generally set payments to start after your sick pay ends, or after any other insurance stops covering you. The longer you wait, the lower the monthly premiums.
- **It covers most illnesses that leave you unable to work** – either in the short or long term (depending on the type of policy and its definition of incapacity).

Vehicle Insurance (must have)

- If you intend to use your own personal vehicle when carrying out property-related business, such as viewing and driving to meetings with potential clients or investors, you must ask your current insurance provider if any amendments are needed to your policy for business use.

Directors' and Officers' (D&O) Liability Insurance (could have)

- Directors' and officers' liability insurance cover offers financial protection to those who are the director, partner or officer of a company. It is designed to cover the cost of claims for compensation made against the insured individual.

Have a good insurance advisor or broker in your power team

- It is advisable to have a very good insurance advisor/broker in your power team, who can advise you on what is required to protect you and your assets. Shop around for the best quotes and weigh up the risks, levels of and cost of the insurance cover.

Lender Consent

- When you are financing any property deal, it is important that the funding type and the property strategy are compatible. For example, a traditional buy-to-let mortgage may not be suitable for an HMO or SA Strategy. If you wish to change your strategy afterwards, always ensure that you have lender approval, and if lender approval cannot be obtained, you would need to look for new funding that is compatible if you wish to proceed with the switch.

Having A Good Letting Agent Can Be A Huge Benefit

As a landlord it is very important to fully understand your responsibilities towards your tenants. Failing to understand, or put in place everything at the start of the tenancy, can prove to be very costly later and mean having to go through a time-consuming, stressful legal process to get your property back. It is one of the reasons why it is well worth getting a good letting agent on a fully managed basis to let and manage your property, as they should have the experience and expertise to ensure that all the correct processes are followed and put in place.

CHAPTER 13

TAX AND FINANCIALS

Property Taxation

The following section is a beginner's guide to property tax and the recent government tax changes affecting the property sector. It is more important than ever to understand what is happening. Taxation is a complex subject and varies depending on everyone's individual circumstances, which is why it is important to get expert advice from a specialist property tax advisor and accountant before starting out. Or, if you have already started, it is essential to understand what options you have to minimise the impact.

There Are Six Main Categories Of Taxes Which Affect Property Taxation:

1. Income Tax.
2. National Insurance Contributions (NIC).
3. Capital Gains Tax (CGT).
4. Stamp Duty Land Tax (SDLT).
5. Inheritance Tax.
6. Corporation Tax.

Depending on your individual circumstances and which structure you are using for your property business, it will affect which type of taxes will apply to you.

There are also several tax allowances which apply in certain circumstances. Having knowledge of these and applying them is where an expert property accountant and tax advisor earn their worth.

The taxes you pay and the allowances that you can apply will depend on which type of structure you use to invest and trade in. It could be:

- Individual sole trader.

- Incorporated as a limited company.
- Or some other more advanced structure, like offshore companies.

Types Of Taxation As An Individual:

- Income Tax.
- National Insurance.
- Capital Gains Tax.
- Stamp Duty.
- Additional Stamp Duty.
- Inheritance Tax.

Types Of Taxation When Trading As A Ltd Company:

- Corporation tax.
- Taxes related hiring employees (If applicable)
- Stamp Duty
- Additional Stamp Duty

Company Structure

Deciding Whether To Invest And Trade As An Individual Or Limited Company.

- Due to recent property taxation changes, the big question on a lot of property investors' minds is whether they should invest in property as an individual sole trader or incorporate as a limited company.
- There are advantages and disadvantages to both, which will depend on everyone's individual circumstances.
- Do not listen to anyone who says there is a one size fits all strategy. Seek out the best advice, as this area can have a large impact on your profits and financial wealth.

Main Factors To Consider When Choosing To Trade As Individual Or Ltd Company:

- What is your current personal tax situation?

- What are your future goals?
- What allowances will you be able to claim?
- What expenses will you be able to claim?
- Could you spread your tax liability through other people?
- Are you going to be a property trader, investor or both?
- Are you buying with cash, mortgage or other finance?
- Are you buying for long-term investment?
- Are you buying for short-term capital gain?
- What is your risk profile?
- How will the taxman view your status based on your choices?
- Will you need to be VAT registered?
- What is your financial strategy?
- How to mitigate or reduce income tax, capital gains tax, inheritance tax, stamp duty, corporation tax?

Individual Sole Trader

Setting up as a sole trader is one of the easiest things to do in terms of registration and administration requirements. However, there is no legal distinction between the business and the individual owner. This means you are personally responsible for all business debts with no limit on liability. Your home and other assets will be at risk if you are unable to meet your financial obligations. On the positive side, as there is no legal distinction between your personal finances and business finances, there is no need to go through any complex procedures to remove money for personal use, which can be a benefit when refinancing property.

Limited Company

A limited company is one of the most popular business structures for all sizes of organisation. This is due to some benefits that it provides over other types of legal business structures. Below is a brief overview of some of the advantages and disadvantages of forming a limited company, compared to trading as an individual sole trader.

Advantages Of Trading As A Ltd Company:

The main reasons for incorporating and trading as limited company are limited liability, tax efficiency and professional status.

- Minimising personal liability.
- Separate legal identity.
- Professional status.
- Credibility and trust.
- Tax efficiency and planning.
- Higher personal remuneration.
- Splitting income.
- Investment and lending opportunities.
- Protecting a company name.
- Easier to sell/transfer business ownership.
- May be easier to access finance.
- Pension.

An Example Of Tax Efficiency:

One of the key advantages of a limited company is financial; the tax efficiencies associated with a limited company can make it the most profitable, and tax efficient, way to run your business. If you are earning more than £35,000 a year, then it can be beneficial to take your remuneration as a combination of salary and dividends.

For example, if you pay yourself a salary of £8,000 and a dividend of £32,000 in the 2018/19 tax year, as your salary falls within the personal allowance there's no income tax to pay, and because you earn less than £155 a week, you won't pay national insurance.

You will also be able to add the £3,850 of your unused personal allowance to your £2,000 dividend allowance, letting you take £5,850 of your dividend tax-free.

The remaining £28,150 is taxed at 7.5pc, giving a tax charge of £1961.25, meaning you take home £38,038.75 of your £40,000 earnings.

Even taking in to account the £6,400 of corporation tax paid by the company on the dividend into account, it would still leave you with more take home pay than a sole trader earning the same amount.

Disadvantages of a limited company

As you would expect with anything that provides many benefits, there are also some disadvantages:

- Must be officially incorporated at Companies House.
- Company name is subject to certain restrictions.
- Not suitable for undischarged bankrupts or disqualified directors.
- Required to disclose personal and corporate information on public record.
- More complex and time-consuming accounting requirements.
- Likely need to appoint an accountant to help you with your tax affairs.
- Strict procedures for withdrawing money from the business.
- A confirmation statement and annual accounts must be filed at Companies House each year.
- Must send a company tax return and annual accounts to HMRC every year.
- Must adhere to strict record keeping requirements.
- A number of company registers and records must be maintained and made available for public inspection at your registered office.
- If you make any changes to your company details, you must notify Companies House immediately.

Before you start property investing and/or trading, get expert advice on which structure will be the most tax efficient and beneficial for you in reaching your investment, financial and wealth goals.

CHAPTER 14

DEVELOPING A MILLIONAIRE MINDSET

Millionaires and self-made wealthy people think differently to those who are poor or stuck in a lower or middle-income range.

In order to achieve the level of financial independence and freedom that you have been dreaming about, it is essential to develop and adopt a 'millionaire mindset'. Without it, you will remain stuck where you are, going around and around in circles or spinning your wheels, and remaining in the same position. We cannot expect to achieve a different result if we keep repeating the same actions.

Most people who look at the lives of those who are successful, underestimate the value of talent, work ethic and mindset in their successes, and overestimate the value of luck. There is no such thing as good or bad luck. We make our own luck. In order to achieve success, it is essential to take 100% responsibility for our own life, and drop any victim mentality. Life is always happening for us, not to us.

> *"When We Change The Way We Look At Things And*
> *Our View Of The World, The Things We Look At And*
> *The World Around Us Changes."*
> **– Calum Kirkness**

Many wealthy people and self-made millionaires drive used cars, live in average neighbourhoods, wear average-priced clothes, watches and accessories and are very careful with their money. If you follow some of the rich and famous, you will be able to see that this is the case. There is a big difference between those who are rich and those who *look* rich!

Your job is to learn and adopt the knowledge, mindset and habits of a millionaire mindset and become one of those people who are genuinely rich. Anyone can become rich with the right mindset.

In Order To Understand The Difference Between The Wealthy And Poor, There Are A Few Key Differences:

- The wealthy understand the difference between assets and liabilities. Where assets produce an income and or increase in value over time and liabilities cost money and or decrease in value over time.
- The wealthy understand the effects of leveraging their time and money and when and how to use it for maximum effect.
- The wealthy understand the power of the compound effect.
- The wealthy understand that everything is energy. Positive thoughts exude positive emotions, which attract positive people, opportunities and outcomes.
- The wealthy understand the importance of the people they surround themselves with. Positive people encourage growth and are happy for other people's success, whilst negative people have a problem for everything.
- The wealthy understand the importance of their environment and the places they spend time in. Our environment has a big impact on our wellbeing. Being in a natural or positive environment is beneficial to the results that you can achieve.
- The wealthy understand how their minds work. We are not our thoughts and we can control how much attention we give to them.
- The wealthy understand that time is our most precious commodity and valuable asset, and therefore understand the importance of how to manage it.

Another important wealth factor to understand and assess is your current financial comfort zone. Think of it in the same way as how the central heating system in your house operates, where the thermostat will come on when the temperature becomes too low and/or switch off when the temperature gets too high. The same is true with your level of wealth thermostat (comfort zone around money).

When you feel uncomfortable with having too little money in your bank account or too much debt, you will start to save until the level gets back within your financial comfort zone; when you have more money or wealth than you are comfortable with, you will spend some money until your bank balance falls back into your financial comfort zone. You might not even have been aware of this until someone highlights it to you, as it usually all happening without your conscious awareness. It is the reason why so many lottery winners end up back where they were before their win.

If you don't work on developing a millionaire mindset by retraining or reprogramming your subconscious mind with its negative attitudes and limiting beliefs towards money and wealth, you will remain stuck where you are.

How To Develop A Millionaire Mindset

Let's look at how you can learn the secrets of the millionaire mind and what steps you need to take for it to become your reality.

Replacing Limiting Beliefs With Positive Ones

First, you must identify your limiting beliefs around money in order to release them.

Some Common And Typical Limiting Beliefs Are:

- Money is the root of all evil.
- Money doesn't grow on trees.
- You must have money to make money.
- You must work too hard to make a lot of money.
- You can't buy happiness.
- The more money you have, the more problems you have.
- I don't have what it takes to make a lot of money.
- I can make money, but I can't seem to hold onto it.
- Money is not that important. It's only money.
- Money is there to be spent.
- The rich get richer and the poor get poorer.
- I'm just not good with money.
- My family has never been rich.

If you are to become financially free and build wealth for your freedom and security, it is essential that you must replace any limiting beliefs and develop a millionaire mindset. Money on its own is not bad. It is the interpretation and use of it by some people that can make it appear bad. The opposite is true and it can be used for a lot of good.

When we look at the behaviour and approach of those who are financially successful and those who struggle to create wealth, there are several key differences.

Comparison Of A Successful Mindset vs. An Unsuccessful Mindset:

Success Mindset (Growth Mindset)	Unsuccessful Mindset (Fixed Mindset)
Abundant mindset	Scarcity mindset
Embrace change	Fear change
Want others to succeed	Secretly hope others fail
Manage their time well	Always busy but unproductive
Accept responsibility failures	Blame others
Exude joy	Exude anger
Talk about ideas	Talk about people
Share information	Hoard information
Give credit to others	Take all the credit
Set goals	Don't set goals
Write down their plans	Have no plans
Keep a journal	Don't keep a journal
Read books	Watch TV
Transformational perspective	Transactional perspective
Continuously learning	Think they know it all already
Complement others	Criticise others
Forgive others	Hold grudges
Have gratitude	Have a sense of entitlement
Associate with positive people	Associate with negative people
Patient	Impatient

Developing a millionaire mindset takes time and patience to develop, and requires an open mind and effort.

Growth is one of our basic human needs. When we ignore our need and drive for growth, we slowly go in to decline, which is in effect, slowly dying. Have you ever watched how quickly some people deteriorate once they retire if they do not replace their employment with some other form of activity or interest? I am sure you have seen it happen. So even when you have reached a level of financial freedom, it is important that you maintain a growth mindset to keep you young in body, mind and spirit.

In most cases people become wealthy over a long period of time and it is based on slow, incremental growth, resulting from smart use of leveraging and the compound effect.

The next time you think that an action is too small to be taken, or a goal is too far away to achieve, think about the compound effect. Below are some examples of the power of the compound effect:

The Snowball Effect

You may have heard the compound effect described as the snow ball effect. The snowball effect is a metaphor for compounding, and it demonstrates how small actions repeated over time can lead to big results. When you make a snowball in your hands and start rolling it down a hill, with each revolution the snowball gathers more and more snow, and by the time it reaches the bottom of the hill it has grown into a large snow boulder.

1 Pence To 1 Million In Under One Month!

Another example that illustrates the power of the compound effect is if you take 1p today and double it each day, you will be a millionaire in less than one month. That rate of growth and doubling every day would be very hard to achieve, but even a small percentage difference in the discount that you can negotiate in deals, and generally being efficient in everything that you do, all compounds over time into making a big difference.

One final example:

£10 To £1 Million In One Round Of Golf!

Imagine you are out for a round of golf with your friend and to add a little extra competition and spice to the match, you agree to play for some money. The rule is that you will start and play the first hole for £10. Then each hole you play, the money doubles.

Hole 1 = £10, hole 2 = £20, hole 3 = £40, hole 4 =£80, hole 5 = £160, hole 6 = £320, hole 7 = £640, hole 8 = £1280, hole 9 = £2560, hole 10- = £5120, hole 11 = £10,240, hole 12 = £20,480, hole 13 = £40,960, hole 14 = £81,920, hole 15 = £163,840, hole 16 = £327,680, hole 17 = £655,360, hole 18 = £1,310,720.

You can see the incredible power of understanding the compound effect and having it work in your favour. One small action today, repeated consistently and frequently, can build momentum and have a great effect.

When you borrow money to buy liabilities (bad debt), that is the compound effect working in reverse against you. It's like starting at the 18th hole and working your way back to the 1st.

Millionaire Mindset Rules:

- Develop the habits and mindset of the wealthy people shared above.
- Focus on achieving and getting what you want.
- Become goal-oriented.
- Don't worry about the competition – winners focus on winning, losers focus on winners.
- Look at ways to increase your knowledge – the best investment that you can ever make is in yourself.
- Look at ways to increase your income without losing any time.
- Don't spend your money – carefully consider every expenditure. Remember the power of saving a little each day and the compound effect can work in both directions.

- Save and invest your money – stop working for your money (selling your time for money) and make your money work for you.
- Be patient – never allow yourself to feel that a financial investment decision is urgent and must be made immediately.
- Due diligence – the wealthy understand the importance of due diligence and the value of getting expert advice.
- Think big – start off with small goals and use your millionaire mindset, leverage and the compound effect to achieve big results.
- Take responsibility for your future – push hard enough for anything and you will achieve your goals.
- Protect your assets – as you begin to accumulate money and assets, adopt a wealthy habit of protecting them.

Do Not Take Advice From Anyone Who Hasn't Done What You Would Like To Do, And Be Careful When Taking Advice From Second Generation Wealth.

There will be people on your journey who will try to hold you back; you will have haters as you make progress on your journey to success. As you grow, others will become jealous and some might try to pull you back. Look on jealousy from others as a sign that you are growing.

If anyone takes up space in your mind with negative thoughts, evict them immediately. If they refuse to leave, increase the rent immediately until they can no longer afford to live there!

> *"Life Is Magical, Not Logical. If Your Dreams Are Logical, They Are Not Big Enough. Dream Big And When You Believe In Yourself And Believe In Your Dreams, The Magic Will Start To Happen."*
> **– Calum Kirkness**

Something Even More Important Than The Millionaire Mindset:

The most important part of the process is the person that you must become in terms of courage, character, thoughtfulness and persistence in achieving your goals. As you progress on your journey towards your goals and achieving them, you will increasingly feel happier and satisfied with yourself and fulfilled. This is the most important and worthwhile goal of all.

Start To Practise Acting As If You Were A Millionaire Now.

Practise the principle of acting "as if." Start right now and act how you would if you were already a millionaire or multi-millionaire. How would you talk, walk, dress, hold your body, eat? What would your attitude be? How would you interact with your family, friends, co-workers, clients, and customers? Then, start acting that way today. Stay humble and polite and let your actions and results do most of the talking. Until you get to where you would like to be, think to yourself: how would the person you would like to be do the things you are about to do?

The more you practise these habits daily, the more confident, outgoing, happier, enthusiastic and energetic you will feel, which will help you attract the people, resources, and opportunities to create the life of your dreams.

Write down how much money you are going to make within the next year and make a note to pay yourself that sum on the date you set.

> *"Believe In Yourself: Believe In Your Dreams."*
> **– Calum Kirkness**

CHAPTER 15

CREATING YOUR PROPERTY BUSINESS PLAN

For a plan to be effective, it is essential to have a clear vision of what you want to achieve.

Being clear on what you want to accomplish is an essential part of putting together your property investment and business plan. More people know what they don't want rather than what they do want. They know they don't want to spend another day in the rat race, or that they need to take responsibility for their financial position in retirement. Successful property investors know exactly what they want to accomplish.

For A Plan To Be Effective:

- It is essential that you have a clear vision of what you want to achieve. If you do not know where you are going, how can you ever know how to get there and even if you do get there, you won't know that you have arrived!
- Begin with the end in mind, and then reverse engineer it by breaking it down into small, manageable and measurable tasks.
- Keep it short, concise, clear, easy to understand, implement, track, measure.

Reverse Engineer Your Goals And Keep It Simple.

As I have grown older I have become a big believer in keeping things simple. So, I will also keep this section, short, concise, clear, easy to understand and implement so that you can put together a plan that is easy for you to track, measure and achieve your desired goals.

> *"It Is Much Easier To Make Something Complicated Than*
> *It Is To Keep It Simple."*
> **– Calum Kirkness**

To get from where we are to where we want to be, there are four key things that we need to know and understand:

1. Where we are at now.
2. Where we would like to be.
3. When you want to be there.
4. How and what we need to get from where we are to where we want to be.

Think of developing your plan in the same way as programming the satellite navigation system in your car. You are setting out on a journey to somewhere you want to go but don't know the directions of how to get you there.

Once the GPS system knows where you are and where you want to go, it will give you the directions one step at a time and let you know the anticipated time of arrival. When you focus on the instruction you will stay on track, when you don't you will end up taking wrong turnings and getting lost! Your intuition is always guiding you. Trust it and if you really want to accelerate your journey and stay on track, the best way is to get a coach or mentor.

It is important that you enjoy the journey. If you don't, you are unlikely to enjoy the destination and end up sabotaging your success when you reach there.

"It Is Important That You Enjoy The Journey To The Destination, Otherwise You Will Subconsciously Sabotage Your Success Once You Arrive."
– Calum Kirkness

Once you know where you are and where you want to go, you can begin to make a plan of how to get you there and which vehicle you need. Only you know where you want to go. The best way to do this is to break down the goals into bite-sized chunks, which are easy to understand and achieve. Set yourself S.M.A.R.T goals. SMART describes how to set SPECIFIC,

MEASUREABLE, ATTAINABLE, REALISTIC and TIMELY goals.

How To Put Your Property Plan Together:

1. Select, write down and master your chosen property strategy.
2. Select, write down and master your prime location and goldmine area.
3. Select, define and write down your niche that you are going to focus on, and master.
4. Select and write down your ideal tenant, guest or buyer.
5. Select and build your power team.
6. Select and write down your ideal property type.
7. Select and write down your ideal property size.
8. Select and write down your ideal property condition.
9. Select and write down your sourcing plan.
10. Select and write down your marketing plan.
11. Select and write down your investment criteria.
12. Select and write down the permissions and protections that you will need for your strategy.
13. Develop, write down and master your due diligence criteria and system.
14. Select and write down your property business structure, i.e. trade as individual or company.
15. Identify your funding requirements, options and availability
16. Write down your strengths and weaknesses.
17. FOCUS, FOCUS, FOCUS!
18. ACTION, ACTION, ACTION!

"You Will Never Gain Total Clarity Through Thinking And Planning Alone. You Must Begin The Journey And Most Of Your Clarity Will Come From The Action You Take As You Go Along."
– Calum Kirkness

Your Five-Year Plan:

Develop a five-year plan. Take some time to think about how your perfect day would be and imagine that you are living and experiencing it now, all the way down to the finest detail. Write it down including the top five major goals that you are going to achieve. When you are preparing your five-year plan, dream big and don't worry about the how at this stage! If you can dream it, you can achieve it! Regularly read your notes on your perfect day.

Once you have written down your vision of the future and your ideal day, calculate the monthly cost of sustaining that lifestyle.

Prepare a vision board with your five-year goals on it, and make the pictures as specific as possible to what you want to achieve. Keep it in a highly visible place where you will see it regularly.

Break Down Your Five Year Vision Plan Into Smaller Plans:

- **Year One Plan** – Develop your year one plan and break it down in to monthly goals that will move you closer to your major goals.
- **Monthly Action Plan** – Develop a monthly plan for each month in year one, setting out how you will achieve your one big goal each month. Calculate how much you need to make during the month to keep you on track to meet your goals.
- **Weekly Plan** – Develop a weekly plan before the week starts, which focuses on achieving one to three goals each week, which moves you closer to your bigger goals.
- **Daily Plan** – Develop a daily plan which you write down the evening before, with one to three key actions that you will take each day to move you closer towards your larger goals.

Print your plans once you have made them and keep them in a highly-visible place where you will frequently see them.

Time Management – Remember the story I shared earlier in the book about having 86,400 seconds in your time account each day; use them wisely, they cannot be carried forward. The people achieving more success than you are simply using these seconds more wisely than you! **Some successful people who have the same 24 hours a day as you do:**

- Warren Buffett
- Tony Robbins
- Jeff Bezos,
- Elon Musk
- Mark Zuckerburg
- Opray Winfrey
- Arianna Huffington
- Jack Ma
- JK Rowling
- Michelle Mone
- Grant Cordone

When you are preparing your daily, weekly, yearly and five-yearly plans, keep in mind:

- S.M.A.R.T Goals.
- Plan – Do – Review – Improve.
- You Can't Master What You Don't Measure.

Once you start, which I would encourage you to do now, it is important that you focus on your goals, your strategy, goldmine area and achieving the results to ensure that you meet your goals. It is important once you have started to keep the momentum going.

If you are not achieving the result that you are looking for, do not adjust and downgrade your goals to meet your plans; upgrade your plans so that you stay on track to achieving your goals.

In the beginning it is important to understand that most people overestimate what they can achieve in the short term, but if you keep going, you realise that you have underestimated what you can achieve over several years.

Do not try to do everything yourself. Think of yourself as the conductor of the orchestra; you do not need to know everything or play every instrument, which is why you build a power team. Nevertheless, it is essential to have a basic knowledge of all areas in order to be able to ask the right questions, to appoint the right specialists and then be able to make an informed decision based on their advice.

"80% Of Your Results Will Come From 20% Of Your Actions. Focus On The Actions That Bring You The Results That You Are Looking For."
– Calum Kirkness

What Now?

I sincerely hope that you have enjoyed reading this book, and will take action to put together your property business plan to build a six, seven or eight figure property investment business that creates financial freedom and allows you to live the live that you desire.

The information and examples shared in this book are based in the UK. However, the fundamentals and principles of property investing are pretty much the same throughout the world. I spend a lot of time in Malaysia and the fundamentals of the property market are the same there and everywhere I go.

Being a property investor and developer can be a lonely journey on your own, which is why I always recommend having a coach and/or mentor to guide and support you. I also recommend being part of a mastermind group. The benefits of being surrounded by like-minded people are huge in terms of support; it will accelerate your route to success and make it more enjoyable.

During the last few years, I was curious as to why so many people attending personal development events were not making any, or only a little, progress despite the investment of their time and money. I looked into the subject in more detail to find out what these people felt was lacking from the seminars and products that they were investing in and I found that the common theme was the seminars talked a lot about 'WHAT TO DO' but they didn't provide the detail on 'HOW TO DO IT' and 'WHY TO DO IT'.

I wanted to create products that give people the whole solution and not just part of the solution, so I have been creating systems that would take beginners and amateurs by the hand and show them:

- How to do it.
- Why to do it.

- In what order to do it.
- How to know if it is working or not.
- What to do if something goes wrong and how to get back on track.

I would like to share details of how I believe I can help you further on your property investment journey to make it smoother, quicker and more enjoyable.

Property Success Insider™ offers the following further resources:

- **Property Success Online** – Online property investment and development training programmes designed to allow you to learn in the comfort of your own home, at a pace that suits you.
- **Live Training Events** – A range of intensive one, three, and five-day property investment and development training events designed to accelerate your property success journey.
- **Mastermind Events** – Regular mastermind meetings are held to bring like-minded people together to share their knowledge.
- **Group Coaching** – Three, six and twelve-month small group coaching programmes are available.
- **Mentoring** – I only offer a few one-to-one mentorship spaces each year, which are by application only.
- **Mastermind Retreats** – Five-day intensive events held in amazing locations around the world.

To find out more and sign-up or apply to join our events and programmes, visit: **www.propertysuccessinsider.com**

BOOK REVIEW REQUEST

PLEASE HELP OTHERS BY SHARING A REVIEW OF THE BOOK ON AMAZON

Printed in Poland
by Amazon Fulfillment
Poland Sp. z o.o., Wrocław

50532682R00117